0723
5/4

# THE
# SECRET
# LANGUAGE
## OF YOUR
# NAME

# THE
# SECRET
# LANGUAGE
## OF YOUR
# NAME

## UNLOCK THE MYSTERIES OF
## YOUR NAME AND BIRTHDATE THROUGH
## THE SCIENCE OF NUMEROLOGY

# Neil Koelmeyer
# & Ursula Kolecki

**ATRIA** PAPERBACK
New York London Toronto Sydney New Delhi

BEYOND WORDS
Hillsboro, Oregon

**ATRIA** PAPERBACK
A Division of Simon & Schuster, Inc.
1230 Avenue of the Americas
New York, NY 10020

BEYOND WORDS
20827 N.W. Cornell Road, Suite 500
Hillsboro, Oregon 97124-9808
503-531-8700 / 503-531-8773 fax
www.beyondword.com

Managing editor: Lindsay S. Brown
Editor: Gretchen Stelter, Jennifer Weaver-Neist
Design: Devon Smith
Proofreader: Jade Chan
Composition: William H. Brunson Typography Services

First Atria Paperback/Beyond Words trade paperback edition March 2012

**ATRIA** PAPERBACK and colophon are trademarks of Simon & Schuster, Inc.
Beyond Words Publishing is a division of Simon & Schuster, Inc.

For more information about special discounts for bulk purchases, please contact Simon & Schuster Special Sales at 1-866-506-1949 or business@simonandschuster.com.

The Simon & Schuster Speakers Bureau can bring authors to your live event.
For more information or to book an event, contact the Simon & Schuster Speakers Bureau at 1-866-248-3049 or visit our website at www.simonspeakers.com.

Manufactured in the United States of America

10 9 8 7 6 5 4 3 2 1

*Library of Congress Cataloging-in-Publication Data*

Koelmeyer, Neil.
    The secret language of your name : unlock the mysteries of your name and birthdate through the science of numerology / Neil Koelmeyer and Ursula Kolecki. — 1st Atria Paperback/Beyond Words trade pbk. ed.
        p.  cm.
    1. Fortune-telling by names.   2.  Names, Personal—Miscellanea.   3.  Fortune-telling by birthdays.
4.  Birthdays—Miscellanea. 5. Numerology. I. Kolecki, Ursula. II. Title.
BF1729.N3K64   2012
133.3'3—dc23
                                                                                    2011041716

    ISBN: 978-1-58270-350-3
    ISBN: 978-1-4516-6601-4 (eBook)

The corporate mission of Beyond Words Publishing, Inc.: *Inspire to Integrity*

*Giving a name, indeed, is a poetic art.*

—Thomas Carlyle

# CONTENTS

# CONTENTS

# INTRODUCTION:
# WHAT IS NUMEROLOGY?

It is generally accepted that Pythagoras introduced the science of numbers to the Western world some 2,400 years ago and that he gained his knowledge of numbers, among many other things, from Egypt and the Near East. Although the roots of the science of numerology are lost in the distant past, some researchers have found evidence that it was practiced in Egypt as far back as 13,000 years ago. Its longevity and constancy gives this fascinating study its credibility and validity, as numerology is based on principles that do not change and that prove themselves over and over again.

What is numerology? Though commonly defined as the esoteric interpretation of numbers, put simply, it is the study of vibration. Numbers are merely symbols of creative forces or vibratory frequencies, having a qualitative value as well as their common quantitative value. In numerology, we are concerned with the qualitative value, the number's vibration, as opposed to the quantitative value.

We may use the terms "number" and "vibration" interchangeably, but numerology is not the study of numbers as such. A number by itself means nothing. It is the vibratory quality and power, positive or negative, symbolized by a number that we weigh and consider. When we think of numbers, we really think in terms of vibratory frequencies that compose and influence both matter and non-matter. Everything that exists is formed and sustained in a vibratory state. In other words, the very nature of the universe is vibratory. Science has proved that all life is motion—motion of universal energy. We call this motion vibration because of its wavelike nature. Every substance, color, shape, smell, and sound is created by vibration. In addition, abstract qualities such as individual characteristics, desires, emotions, and other extrasensory conditions are vibrations.

When we talk about vibration, we also mean number, and each number is a symbol of a particular chain of qualities. Each number from 1 to 9—the symbols of numerology—represents a unique combination of personality characteristics. Particular numbers from our birthdate and name play a prominent role in shaping our personality and destiny. Their effectiveness will depend on their position, their frequency of occurrence, and their relationship with other numbers.

The numbers also describe the potential of our personality. However, it is up to us to choose if we will exploit the talents or overdevelop the negative tendencies of our personality. The numbers describe the essential aspects of our individual characters, but it is up to us to embrace or reject these aspects, deriving benefit from them or abusing them. The quality of leadership, for instance, could be benevolent or dictatorial; business acumen could lead either to greed and ruthless competition or the acquisition of wealth through sound judgment and hard work.

It is important that we understand ourselves and our motivations. No meaningful relationship can be built without a similar appreciation of others and their motivations. A study of numerology may help us recognize the reasons behind the apparently illogical or inexplicable actions of another, or even ourselves, and with this knowledge comes tolerance.

Numerology informs us of our assets and shortcomings so that we can make the best of the former and improve and control the latter. A character analysis using numerology tells us about our general personality traits and our potential strengths and weaknesses. It suggests suitable employment and pastimes and examines how we handle financial resources. It reveals our social habits and reactions in various relationships. Numerology can play a considerable part in establishing a harmonious relationship in one's personal life as well as in business. In all types of relationships, it is helpful to do numerological research on the person or persons involved.

Numerology can help us by providing some insight into the personality, motivations, and likely actions of people. As many of us are not skilled judges of character and wish we had the patience and ability to develop greater psychological intuition, the principles of numerology could aid us in many aspects of human activity.

If people work toward making a positive contribution by pursuing the fulfillment of their destiny, they will be less frustrated and more satisfied with life and reap greater rewards. Numerology can help them achieve this.

There may be conflict between the personality type, the directions of destiny, and the natural talents of an individual. The personality may be dominant and make one hesitate in adapting to meet the requirements of inherent talent and destiny. Or the destiny and talent may pull the person in a certain direction, while the personality may lack the enthusiasm and resources to fulfill that destiny. Recognizing the conflict is halfway to solving the problem, and an objective party, armed with a numerological interpretation, may achieve a breakthrough in understanding.

Lack of harmony within the personality may surface in unsettled and unsuitable behavior. People in guiding roles may develop strategies to address and neutralize these conflicts. This may help their clients or friends gain the personality strength they need to resolve their own dilemmas. Numerology could be one more tool in helping others in their personal healing process.

It is said that we choose our friends but not our relatives. We also can't always choose the people in our workplace, with whom we may find ourselves in conflict on occasion. Numerology can show us how best to deal with these people and encourage a relationship of harmony. Applying what we learn from a numerological perspective does more than help us defuse potential conflict as well; it can also show us how to recognize the assets of individuals and build on them.

A study of numerology will also describe the personality potential of a child and can give us guidance when figuring out the best directions to steer them to fulfill that potential. It can provide some answers as to why children behave in certain ways, and if it is behavior we do not wish to encourage, we may analyze the personality differences between ourselves and our children and try to judge whether the desired behavior is compatible with their personalities or simply something our personalities cause us to prefer. When this knowledge is unearthed and recognized, a greater rapport can be established within the family. We may often set goals for our children that merely reflect our own unfulfilled ambitions. Numerology can help us objectively assess whether their behavior is really unacceptable and deserving of discipline and correction or whether it is behavior we are personally ill equipped to understand and tolerate.

A unique feature of this book is the focus on names and how both birthdate and name affect our lives and our numerological vibrations. Traditional name books focus on the historical meanings taken from, among others, the Celtic, Anglo-Saxon, Scandinavian, Greek, and Latin tongues, and traditional numerology books focus on either birthdates or names, often not explaining their complex interplay.

We would like to suggest that while we may be curious about the historical meanings of names, this knowledge will not be useful to a child. However, if names are chosen with regard to their vibratory powers, keeping in mind their relationship to the birthdate, there is every chance that the characteristics connected to that name's vibration will blossom in a person's personality and support their life path.

The name, especially the given name, plays an important role in balancing and strengthening the features of the child's birthdate. With the help of numerology, parents can choose the name that will have the best possible effect on a child's personality and destiny, and adults can discover the suitability of their own names and those of others in relation to their birthdates. Numerology interprets the fascinating interrelation of these numbers and describes the multidimensional facets of individuality and potential.

The chapters that follow are a step-by-step guide on how to obtain information through numbers and how to gain a good understanding of this information. We examine the six principal Spheres of Influence that combine to form our personality complex. Two of these spheres are found in the birthdate and four in the name. Once a working knowledge of each sphere has been attained, the next step is to learn how to see them all at once. We cannot expect to immediately make wise decisions based on numerological insights, but with patience and enthusiasm we can gain remarkable insights into personality and potential.

This book is designed for the general reader; it is not a definitive textbook. Many intricate aspects of numerology have been intentionally omitted for this reason. For readers keen to develop further knowledge, we recommend continued study accompanied by constant observation of the various vibratory influences on themselves and others.

# 1

---

# THE SIX SPHERES OF INFLUENCE

Before we can gain any significant wisdom from the lessons of numerology, we need to calculate the numbers that mirror the personality, talents, and destiny of the person or persons we wish to study. This section can be used as a quick reference for calculating the numbers of the Six Spheres of Influence. As mentioned in the introduction, the symbols of numerology are the numbers 1 to 9. This means that any number beyond 9 needs to be reduced to a single digit to arrive at the numerological symbol of that number. This is done by simple addition. For example, 33 is 3 + 3 = 6, and 19 is 1 + 9 = 10 and then 1 + 0 = 1. The numerological symbols of 33 and 19 are 6 and 1, respectively. Once the final digit, or numerological symbol, has been determined, we consider its characteristics as well as the characteristics of the numbers that serve to form this digit. There are two exceptions to this rule, however, and these are the numbers 11 and 22. They are known as Master Numbers. When these numbers are found, it is best to reduce them, as 1 + 1 = 2 for the former and 2 + 2 = 4 for the latter. After close examination of the overall chart read in that manner, you may then consider to what extent the qualities of the unreduced Master Numbers influence the personality. More information on these Master Numbers is given below and in chapter 2.

## Master Numbers/Vibrations

Surpassing the vibrations symbolized by the digits 1 through 9 are the two Master Numbers, or Vibrations, 11 and 22. These complex forces require careful interpretation and application (they are, in fact, maximized versions of the 2 and 4 vibrations), and much is demanded of—and awarded to—persons under their influence. Unlike the Third, Fourth, Fifth, and Sixth Spheres, where Master Numbers are reduced to a single digit in their calculations, the First (Personality) Sphere and the Second (Destiny) Sphere experience the maximum strength of 11 and 22 when they appear. (Master Number calculations are discussed further on page 5.)

Here are some examples of birthdates and names that are under the influence of Master Numbers/Vibrations (you will learn how to calculate these later in this chapter as well as in chapter 3):

| **First Sphere** | **Second Sphere** | **Third Sphere** |
| --- | --- | --- |
| 8/**11**/1975 | 3/4/1966 = 29 = **11** | Aurora (**11**/2) |
| 5/**22**/1990 | 12/28/2007 = **22** | Thomas (**22**/4) |

The bearers of 11 and 22 usually fall into three broad categories. First, there is a small minority who are able to contain the high frequencies of a Master Vibration, but they revert from time to time to their base of 2 and 4 to gain some respite from their elevated condition. Second, there are those who function for the most part as superior Two or Four personalities, occasionally reaching their high potential. Last but not least, there are those who remain superior Twos or Fours and may comprise the majority of Eleven and Twenty-Two personalities.

When 11 or 22 appears in the Second Sphere of Influence (Destiny), it is not reduced to a single digit in its calculation. However, few individuals are given the opportunity to reach the elevated heights of these Master Vibrations. Therefore, the single digits 2 and 4 should be taken into serious consideration. When individuals feel a pull toward the powers of these Master Vibrations, they should endeavor to cultivate their attributes. (You can read more on Master Number characteristics on pages 71–78.)

# The Birthdate: First and Second Spheres of Influence

## *First Sphere*

The only important piece of information we need is the birthdate. It is important to know the exact date, as in the following examples:

A.  *5/7/1965*

B.  *2/17/1976*

C.  *1/22/2006*

The First Sphere of Influence is formed and governed by the number or numbers of the day of birth. It indicates an individual's personality. In example A, this sphere is wholly controlled by the 7 vibration. Interpretation of this personality will rely heavily on the characteristics of this number. In example B, we have a double-digit birthday, which indicates that this sphere is controlled by three vibrations. The 17 is reduced to 8, which makes this individual an Eight personality; however, the 1 and 7 vibrations will continue to operate, usually in more observable ways, while the 8 vibration is at work in the background. A careful examination of the three interchanging and interpenetrating vibrations is required here. In example C, the Master Vibration 22 has control over this sphere. Since 22 is a Master Number, caution should be exercised in supposing a 22 individual has all the qualities of that vibration; all the qualities are attained by very few, though their potential always remains. The characteristics of the 4 vibration come into force when those of the 22 are not used.

## Interpretation

The First Sphere of Influence is established on the day we are born and gives us a particular personality type, which is further strengthened or weakened by the numbers of the birth month and year and by the vibrations of the given name—the Third Sphere of Influence. Our success depends on the compatibility and cooperation of our personality type with our other Spheres of Influence. The First Sphere is our stamp of individuality, and so it may be regarded as the most important sphere. The only factor that can, to a degree, inhibit or enhance our personality traits will be the overriding influences of our environment.

This First Sphere is temporarily hidden in our casual meetings, and on these occasions, people encounter the forces of the Sixth Sphere of Influence—the outer person. These forces are not always the same as those forming our essential personality type and may give inaccurate first impressions. The Sixth Sphere can be used, both consciously and unconsciously, to enhance the traits of the First Sphere and advance the possibilities of the Second Sphere of Destiny. It could also be used to conceal and deceive, as the Sixth Sphere is the facade and not the true person. If the same vibration controls the First, Fifth, and Sixth spheres, the individual will be exactly what he or she appears to be.

## *Second Sphere*

To find the number of this sphere, we add up the numbers of the birthdate. This total, which is always a multiple-digit number, is then reduced to a single digit. When the

Master Numbers 11 and 22 appear in the total, they are not reduced any further (though, again, it is important to consider the characteristics of the 2 and 4, respectively, in regard to those situations). The number of this Sphere of Influence is also known as our Destiny Number and plays a significant role in our lives. Using the birthdates above, we find the numbers of the Second Sphere as follows:

| | | | |
|---|---|---|---|
| *5/7/1965* | *5 + 7 + 1 + 9 + 6 + 5 = 33* | → | *3 + 3 = 6* |
| *2/17/1976* | *2 + 1 + 7 + 1 + 9 + 7 + 6 = 33* | → | *3 + 3 = 6* |
| *1/22/2006* | *1 + 2 + 2 + 2 + 0 + 0 + 6 = 13* | → | *1 + 3 = 4* |

In these examples, the numbers 6, 6, and 4, respectively, form the Second Sphere of Influence and represent the Destiny Number. To avoid misinterpretation of this sphere, shortcuts should not be taken to calculate this number. A common mistake is to calculate the single digit of the birthday, month, and year and then add these three numbers together. For example, 2/17/1976 becomes 2 + 8 + 5 = 15 = 6. Though the final number is correct for this example, if any Master Numbers are involved, the calculation may be wrong. For example, with the birthdate 8/15/1961, the incorrect method would give us 8 + 6 + 8 = 22. The correct method is 8 + 1 + 5 + 1 + 9 + 6 + 1 = 31 = 4, which shows that this person does not have a 22 destiny.

If the Master Numbers 11 and 22 appear in the total, they should not be reduced further but recorded and interpreted as such. If they appear in subtotals (which should only occur for name calculations, not birthdate, as all the numbers of the birthdate are added individually for the Second Sphere), they need not be taken into consideration. At the same time, we should remember that people do not consistently live up to the power of these Master Vibrations, and they automatically revert to the influences of the straightforward 2 or 4 vibrations. Therefore, two interpretations are advisable.

## Interpretation

The Second Sphere of Influence, which controls our destiny, is often referred to as our Life Path. The personality is constantly drawn toward the requirements of this sphere. If the personality type formed by the First Sphere is in sympathy with the demands of the Second Sphere (one's destiny), little or no difficulty will be found and a smooth journey can be expected. However, if these two vital spheres are controlled by vibrations of conflicting natures, many adjustments will be needed.

For an instant numerological assessment of a person, the First and Second Spheres suffice in gaining considerable insight into his or her personality and destiny.

# The Whole Name: Third, Fourth, Fifth, and Sixth Spheres of Influence

The next step is to determine the remaining four Spheres of Influence, which are calculated by using the whole name—the given name, the middle name or names, if any, and the surname. In order to do so, we convert the letters of the name to their number values. Each letter of the alphabet has a corresponding numerical value, as shown in the following chart. Here, we use the name **Maria Kay Martinez** to illustrate these spheres.

| 1 | 2 | 3 | 4 | 5 | 6 | 7 | 8 | 9 |
|---|---|---|---|---|---|---|---|---|
| A | B | C | D | E | F | G | H | I |
| J | K | L | M | N | O | P | Q | R |
| S | T | U | V | W | X | Y | Z | |

## *Third Sphere*

This sphere is determined by adding up the numerical value of the letters of the first name. The vibration 6 in this sphere will play a role in influencing Maria's personality and talents.

*M A R I A*
*4 + 1 + 9 + 9 + 1 = 24* ⟶ *2 + 4 = 6*

### Interpretation

The Third Sphere of Influence can be used to powerfully impact all other spheres. It can provide a vibration not found in the birthdate, using its qualities to create balance and further openings for the personality. It can also be used as a connecting link between the First and Second Spheres to enhance the power of a particular talent or to increase the chances of fulfilling the requirements of a certain destiny. The more conscious you are of the influence your given name has upon your personality, the more power the vibration has. This is the secret of its success.

## *Fourth Sphere*

This sphere is found by adding the number values of the letters of the full name. The single-digit numbers are found for each name before combining them, and then again, they are reduced to a single digit to arrive at the final number. The result of the number 5 is a clue to the natural talents and aptitudes that Maria can apply to her career and leisure activities.

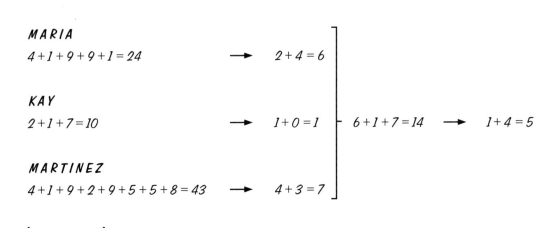

## Interpretation

The Fourth Sphere of Influence reveals the talents we already possess and that can be used in our professions and hobbies. Ideally, these talents will meet the requirements of our destiny and will not conflict with our personality type. If they are in conflict, new talents may need to be developed in order to fulfill our destiny, reserving our existing talents for secondary purposes; this is not uncommon.

## *Fifth Sphere*

This sphere is found by adding the vowels' values from the full name, again reducing each name to a single digit before combining them to find the final number. The vowels *A, E, I, O,* and *U* are converted directly to 1, 5, 9, 6, and 3, respectively. The letter *Y,* which converts to 7, is counted as a vowel if it is found in a position where it functions as a vowel, as in the following instances:

a. When there is no other vowel in the name, as in Flynn or Lynn
b. When there is no vowel in the syllable, as in Tyrone or Sylvia
c. When it is preceded by another vowel and sounded as one, as in Guy or Jayne

In the case of Maria, her inner person will be motivated by the characteristics of the 7 vibration.

$$MA\underline{R}I\underline{A}$$
$$1 + 9 + 1 = 11 \longrightarrow 1 + 1 = 2$$

$$KA\underline{Y}$$
$$1 + 7 = 8$$

$$MA\underline{R}T\underline{I}N\underline{E}Z$$
$$1 + 9 + 5 = 15 \longrightarrow 1 + 5 = 6$$

$$2 + 8 + 6 = 16 \longrightarrow 1 + 6 = 7$$

## Interpretation

The Fifth Sphere of Influence, or inner person, generally plays a concealed role, as the combined forces of the other spheres and environmental influences may relegate it to the background. However, the forces of this sphere do not remain in this position permanently. They emerge from time to time to influence our behavior in long-term affairs, and for this reason, it is essential that this sphere is examined whenever longer-term associations are considered.

## Sixth Sphere

This sphere is found by adding the consonants' values from the full name, again reducing each name to a single digit before combining them to find the final number. Maria's outer personality will display the qualities of the 7 vibration.

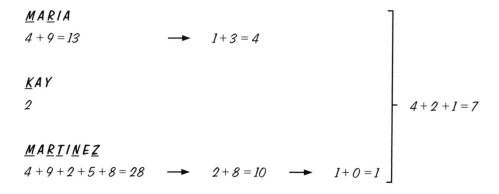

## Interpretation

The Sixth Sphere of Influence is the outer person. We would like to stress that, though its impact is of a temporary nature (one's true personality is revealed from within), it is nevertheless a permanent aspect of our personality. All our first impressions are created and gained through this sphere. It takes center stage whenever we meet people for the first time. It is our prime asset at interviews of any sort. The need to constantly highlight the positive qualities of this sphere and eliminate the negative ones cannot be overemphasized. An unimpressive or disordered outer personality projected through this sphere could do grave injustice to a splendid real personality and vice versa.

# The Spheres Together

The most significant fact that emerges from this brief examination of the six spheres is their interdependence. Our personalities need to function as well-balanced wholes in order for us to answer the call of destiny and make a worthwhile contribution to society. Therefore, all six spheres must be examined for a balanced interpretation of the personality and the degree of influence each sphere has.

An important numerological fact that needs to be considered when examining these spheres is that the unique characteristics of the numbers will remain constant, regardless of the sphere in which they appear. However, they will express themselves differently according to their position in the spheres.

The two Spheres of Influence within the birthdate take precedence over those of the name, as the birthdate is fixed and comprises the mold in which an individual is formed. But the whole name determines the nature of the four other spheres, which are, by contrast, not fixed. In a numerological analysis, it is the given name, the Third Sphere of Influence, that takes the highest priority due to its malleable nature. The vibration of the given name has direct bearing on the First and Second Spheres; its influence can add harmony or conflict to the personality, and it contributes, along with the other names, toward forming the Fourth, Fifth, and Sixth Spheres of Influence.

An assessment of the numbers of all six Spheres of Influence provides a fascinating mix of abilities, attitudes, ambitions, potential, emotions, and conflicts. Numbers may be compatible and bring harmony or in conflict and cause divisions within the personality. Some numbers may neutralize each other, while the power of others may simply be overwhelmed. Our ultimate aim should be to see all six spheres at once, but we want to concentrate on the significance of each sphere and the circumstances in which one or more takes precedence over others. Eventually, we will realize the nature of the astonishing and elusive phenomenon we call the personality complex.

*The web of our life is of a mingled yarn, good and ill together.*

Change "life" to "personality" in this quote from William Shakespeare and it summarizes the complex interrelation of the spheres.

# 2

---

# THE FIRST SPHERE OF INFLUENCE: SPHERE OF PERSONALITY

## The Number or Numbers of the Birthday

In terms of strength and influence, the number or numbers of the day of birth are the most significant. These numbers or vibrations form the personality type and are the First Sphere of Influence. Someone born on the 7th day of any month will possess the properties of the 7 vibration and may be regarded, by and large, as a Seven personality. A multiple-digit birthday, such as the 25th, will also produce a Seven personality, but this individual will not be a straightforward Seven as the 2 and 5 vibrations will constantly influence the 7. A correct assessment of this birthday will include the interpretation of a set of three vibrations. For the most part, the 2 and 5 vibrations will operate in the observable part of the personality, while the 7 will be the foundation. In other words, in a single-digit birthday, personal characteristics are concentrated and in a multiple-digit birthday they are a bit more complex to interpret.

Some degree of caution and skill is needed to interpret a multiple-digit birthday, owing to the constant interplay of three equally strong vibrations. After careful analysis, a person may begin to appreciate which number in the birthdate influences what aspects of the personality. Some aspects of an individual's personality may be compounded when the numbers magnify specific characteristics. Any similarities between characteristics of numbers in a multiple-digit birthday should be looked for. It should also be noted that the repetition of traits and the repetition of the same number in a birthdate will multiply the strength of their influence—positive or negative.

In this chapter, each number or vibration is examined concerning the following:

- Distinguishing Traits
- Possible Positive and Negative Characteristics
- Behavior in Social Situations
- Financial Outlook
- Career Prospects
- Romantic Relationships
- Compatibility
- Childhood
- Best Days
- Style and Colors
- Stones

## Vibration Number 1

The vibration number 1 is the active part of the two primeval vibrations. It represents beginnings, especially of physical life, and is the prime motivator of all other vibrations. An abundance of the number 1 can increase the strength of another vibration considerably, in a powerful and positive way. However, there is a point where the dominance of this number turns an individual to negative forms of expression. Note that it is the only number that determines whether personality traits are used in a positive or negative manner. The degree in which positive and negative qualities are active depends on the frequency of the 1 in the birthdate and name. More information on this aspect of the 1 vibration's influence is given in chapter 5, under the heading "Negativity."

People born on the 1st and 10th may regard themselves as straightforward One personalities. Those born on the 19th are also strong One personalities, with this vibration operating in the observable part of the personality as well as behind the scenes. However, the personality will be heavily tempered by the power of the 9 vibration. The 28th also produces One personalities with little or no conflict between the three vibrations that control the personality, as many of the One qualities are tempered by the 2 and others are enhanced by the powerful 8.

The 1 vibration also appears in birthdates on the 11th, 12th, 13th, 14th, 15th, 16th, 17th, 18th, 21st, 29th, and 31st days of the month. Although these days do not produce One personalities, the influence of the 1 vibration is strong and many of its characteristics should be taken into consideration, especially those of self-confidence and leadership.

## Distinguishing Traits

attentiveness
ability to work under stress
quick recuperative powers
pragmatism
long memory
strong opinions

This primeval vibration produces the genuine nonconformist. Those strongly influenced by it are rigid in their down-to-earth views, especially if supported by a 4 vibration.

## Possible Positive Characteristics

individuality

independence

self-reliance

leadership skills

inventiveness

ambition

authority

determination

courage

vital energy

loyalty

## Possible Negative Characteristics

low self-esteem

poor sportsmanship (especially on the losing end)

sensitivity to criticism and contradiction

excessive ego

boastfulness

pride

irritability

impatience

vanity

narrow-mindedness

obstinacy

dictatorial nature

self-centeredness

indecisiveness

One personalities can be lacking in

adaptability

verbal communication skills

emotional expression

cooperation

tact

patience

humility

listening skills

the ability to laugh at oneself

Their refusal to admit an error may also lead them to go to absurd lengths to justify their words and actions.

## Behavior in Social Situations

Ones do not stand out as conversationalists but enjoy person-to-person communication on subjects of their own preference in which their activities and interests figure largely. They instantly withdraw from frivolous, general conversation in a large group, and the pronouns "I," "me," or "mine" are constantly used in thought and speech and reflect their general "me first" and "me only" attitudes.

The power of the 1 vibration is contained in their written words rather than their spoken words. Gathering a personal following comes easily for them, as does having their ideas copied or followed by others. They expect others to defer to them and may display agitation if this is not done. A subtle approach rather than a head-on confrontation should be used with these personalities.

If not softened by a more flexible number in the other spheres, Ones might live in the extremes of a black-and-white world, without the ability to see the shades of gray.

## Financial Outlook

One personalities establish financial security early in life with their good values. As they do not enjoy luck in the generally accepted way, they make their own path. Motivated by a strong physical vibration, Ones are sensitive to their physical environment and do not hesitate to spend their resources on personal luxuries, as they derive extraordinary satisfaction and pride from a sense of ownership. At the same time, they are discriminating buyers who do not buy on impulse. They are normally quick to pay off loans.

## Career Prospects

In public life, they succeed and thrive in positions demanding

  leadership
  originality
  initiative
  independence
  freedom in decision making

Ones are at their best in positions of authority or in self-employment. They function poorly as subordinates because they resent interference and would rather give orders than take them. In all other affairs, they are givers rather than receivers. As the primeval vibration concerned with outgoing tendencies, subjects of this vibration are still unaware of the opposite force—receiving—which becomes operative with the number 2; the law of attraction is not in effect for this number. Consequently, Ones are happier when they acquire their needs entirely through their own efforts. They do not like being placed under obligation to others by receiving favors and gifts.

Owing to the natural tendency of One personalities toward decision making, they should avoid equal partnerships, since the balance and cooperation needed in such situations will be upset. They work with concentration and intensity and greatly resent interference.

## Romantic Relationships

As companions, Ones naturally take the leading role and can be quite demanding without realizing it. Their habit of intense concentration can make them look stern or even appear indifferent to their surroundings. This is, in fact, not true. It may take some time to understand that they are not intentionally shutting out those around them and that this habit of concentration and single-mindedness is a natural part of their individuality and contains no unkindness.

They are loyal and protective marriage partners who will fight hard to save a marriage facing problems. They will not easily give up on the responsibility of a commitment, especially concerning marriage and family. Separation and divorce are not considered solutions. Natural self-restraint and trouble with emotional expression make them unromantic partners, but their love is deep and abiding. They are not flirtatious and do not tolerate competition in love, and their devotion is displayed by deeds rather than talk.

Their partners need to be compromising, unselfish, patient, and devoted, as Ones are strongly resentful of demanding companions. They are dependable providers and firmly maintain the role of head of the family, regardless of whether they are a wage earner or homemaker, while demanding loyalty and love in return. An outsider's insult or injury to a member of the family will rarely be forgotten or forgiven. They are totally devoted to the welfare of their children, and their partners are often obliged to take second place to this devotion. Their long memories are used both in positive and negative ways, not only in family affairs but in all their activities. Although they give their families the strongest support possible, Ones are career people rather than domestic. They are likely to experience extreme restlessness if they are confined to family duties.

## Compatibility

The best partners for these people are those strongly influenced by the 2 vibration. Such a partnership will provide a good balance of active and receptive contributions, as the 2 is the receptive part of the primeval vibrations. They get on best with Two, Four, Seven, and Eight personalities.

## Childhood

As children, One personalities will display the typical 1 qualities of independence, willpower, determination, individuality, self-reliance, and leadership. Parents and guardians should recognize and appreciate these traits, as well as the creative mental activities of such children, and provide them with opportunities to develop in ways that will give full expression to their creative talents.

Family and social restrictions may inhibit One children during the vital years of growth and force them into negative avenues of expression, such as insubordination, obstinacy, introversion, and leading others in antisocial behaviors. They could be resentful of correction and be domineering, uncooperative, and rough in speech and manner. Fear of losing their individuality may bring about a lack of consideration for others. They should be encouraged to maintain their individuality while also being shown that it is possible to maintain individuality within a group.

Ones are quick to recover from the trauma of a broken home and will be the first to take over responsibility of younger children or even become the new providers. They will usually leave home early, even a well-established one, due to their spirit of independence and adventure. Family loyalty, however, will always remain strong.

## Best Days

Sundays and Mondays are the best days for Ones, especially if these days fall on the 1st, 10th, 19th, or 28th of any month.

## Style and Colors

The 1 vibration symbolizes the sun, whose golden rays have a powerful influence on all One personalities; this also accounts for Ones' extraordinary love of sunshine. Gold is another important symbol of this vibration, and it is also a suitable color for Ones, along with yellow, bronze, golden browns, copper, apricot, flame, orange, and all colors of autumn.

## Stones

The best stones are topaz (yellow), turquoise, amber, ruby, and other stones of these colors. All their jewels should be set in gold.

## *Vibration Number 2*

The 1 vibration on its own is incomplete and unproductive until it is polarized into equal forces with the 2. This division results in the forming of active and receptive vibrations, and their subsequent interaction is the basis of all creation. The number 2 symbolizes the receptive pole. While motivation and action are the basic forces of the

1, receptivity and conservation of power form the nature of the 2. Whereas the 1 represents individuality, the 2 represents associations, partnerships, and union. In more basic terms, the 1 stands for the principle of the provider and the 2 stands for the principle of the keeper.

People born on the 2nd and 20th are true Two personalities, while those born on the 11th and 29th revert to the influence of the 2 vibration if they do not maintain the high octaves of the Master Number 11. Although not producing straightforward Two personalities, this vibration also significantly influences those born on the 12th or from the 21st to 28th of any month.

## Distinguishing Traits

concern with personal welfare

sacrifice of time and energy for others

desire for attention and appreciation

emotionality

awareness

understanding

supportive nature

comforting instincts

warm personality

sympathetic ear

## Possible Positive Characteristics

gentleness

persuasion

patience

impartiality

tact

diplomacy

self-sacrifice

selflessness

romanticism

gallantry

charm

courteousness

thoughtfulness

grace

cooperation

## Possible Negative Characteristics

uncertainty

changeability

oversensitivity

self-consciousness

self-deprecation

timidity

fear of others' opinions

fear of failure

procrastination

shyness

indecision

depression

hypochondria

loneliness
emotional overreaction

Twos often need to develop more

self-assertiveness
self-confidence
objectivity
logic
independence

## Behavior in Social Situations

People with a Two personality are persuasive rather than aggressive and can tone down aggressiveness in others with their gentle approach. They are known for their winning ways and their refined, genteel natures. But they also obscure the great strength of character they possess by appearing weak-willed, expressing their opinions in a round-about manner by saying one thing when they mean another; they resent being cornered into giving a firm opinion. Many people are attracted to Two personalities, and Twos have an aura that frequently draws gifts and offers of help from others. They are the true collectors, not only of physical things but also of facts and figures.

All Two personalities possess a powerful imagination that is more whimsical than creative. They are also known for their psychic ability and extrasensory perception, unless these gifts have been suppressed in their upbringing. This is an uncompetitive vibration, as Two personalities are more concerned with participation than winning. Their strongest desire is for a peaceful lifestyle. If they do not find this, they will withdraw into a private world of fantasy. In order to bring out their best qualities, they need a harmonious and peaceful atmosphere, whether in the domestic scene or elsewhere. They are instantly inhibited by disharmony. Their nervous systems are easily damaged by a life filled with discord, tension, uncleanliness, and ugliness.

The moon is the symbol of the 2 vibration, and individuals strongly influenced by this number have their moods attuned to the phases of the moon. They are generally night people who sleep in during the day.

Twos are extroverts who need social life and company. Those strongly subject to this vibration may appear to be slightly lost or dreamy in aspect. They are not solo performers and feel more comfortable being part of a group, though they prefer to remain on the fringe of activity, rather than become the center of attention. Twos relate better to those who are younger or older than they are; they are too sensitive to keep up with the pressure of handling their contemporaries. Close and long-term friendships are found in this vibration.

## Financial Outlook

Financial security is important to the well-being of Two personalities, but others must provide this, as Twos do not persistently pursue financial gain. They are generous with their money and enjoy giving gifts as much as they enjoy receiving tokens of affection.

## Career Prospects

These personalities work best as partners, seconds-in-charge, and deputies and subordinates. Their talents are displayed while assisting, cooperating, and carrying out the plans of others, rather than originating and directing their own. They are not meant for manual labor and are in their element in occupations where movement is involved, such as travel and communication. Most Twos have a natural urge to follow some form of medical or healing practice. They are also successful in any job that requires precision and delicacy of touch.

## Romantic Relationships

People with a Two personality fall in love easily. They make excellent marriage partners, provided they are not negative Twos, as the type of negativity produced by the 2 vibration can make these personalities quite burdensome. The average Two is prepared to play a backup role in marriage and is best when married to an assertive personality or one controlled by active vibrations. A domestic life free from tension and financial worries is essential. Without romance and variety in marriage, Twos could be tempted to look elsewhere, especially if they do not receive the constant love and attention they need. They show a dislike for argument and will go to great lengths to avoid such situations, even to the extent of subordinating and compromising their own views.

There is a waywardness in the emotional life of Twos. They are easily won over by consideration and other romantic approaches such as frequent—but not necessarily costly—tokens of affection. Partners of these people who recognize this need and pander to their sentimental natures receive a good deal in return. Given love and security, the strength of the Two will flourish and be a tower of strength for their partners. Maternal instinct is strong, and anyone under a Two's influence will receive mothering.

## Compatibility

These personalities get on best with Ones, Sevens, Fours, and Eights.

## Childhood

Children with Two personalities will display adverse reactions to noise or a discordant and inharmonious environment. They enjoy living in a fantasy world of their own, and this may be carried well into adulthood. Sensitivity and shyness will always be problems, especially in their school days. Peace and harmony at home is vital for the development of these children. They can easily develop a variety of strange inhibitions and complexes under callous or neglectful treatment by parents, guardians, and brothers and sisters. These complexes could remain and become serious personality problems as they mature into adults. They are gentle-natured and need the society of children who share their own refined manners. These children may suffer adversely from the result of a broken home and the events that lead up to it. They are sentimental and cry easily. These children are not aggressive and should not be pushed into competitive sports.

Owing to the natural rhythm in their bodies and minds, they take to swimming, dancing, acrobatics, and any other sport where rhythmic and fluid movements are essential. They are true water babies and their natural love of water, especially the sea and other large bodies of water, will remain throughout their lives. The 2 vibration's talent for the written word will be seen in these children at an early stage. It must be recognized that these children have great talent and goodness, which will blossom only in the right environment. Corporal punishment, even of the mildest sort, will have unfortunate and lasting effects on them.

## Best Days

Sundays, Mondays, and Fridays, especially if they fall on the 2nd, 11th, 20th, or 29th of any month, are the best days for Twos.

## Style and Colors

Genuine Two personalities look and feel their best in soft, flowing clothes. Strict business suits are not their style, nor are loud and showy fabrics and designs. Pale colors are most suitable in dress and surroundings. White and lighter shades of green, cream, salmon, blue, and aquamarine should be used. Dark colors should be avoided.

## Stones

Twos' stones are pearls, moonstones, and pale green stones set in silver.

# *Vibration Number 3*

The fusion of the active 1 and receptive 2 vibrations brings forth the number 3. This vibration stands for the principle of youth and possesses inherited traits of its parentage (the 1 and 2) as well as distinct qualities of its own, thus giving it a wide range of motivation and expression. It is the first vibration that contains a mixture of both active and receptive attributes, with the active elements predominating.

The 3rd and 30th days of any month, as well as the 12th and 21st, produce Three personalities. While individuals born on the 3rd and 30th have unmixed 3 characteristics, they will need the 1 vibration in a degree of strength in the rest of their birthdate or names in order to keep on the positive side of this vibration. Those with the 12th or 21st as their birthday are already positive personalities and will be able to develop the best 3 qualities lying in the background of their personalities.

It is an extrovert vibration and, true to its youthful nature, the zest for living and self-expression are the dominant forces governing those it strongly influences. Concern for self and self-interests are prominent features, as in the case of the One and Two personalities.

## Distinguishing Traits

good manners
tact
charm
effervescence
enthusiasm
leadership skills
authority
versatility
eternal youthfulness
vitality
easy self-expression
exceptionally high intelligence
acute sense of accuracy
perfectionism

The Three's engaging lifestyle keeps its bearers looking younger than their actual years, and their need for artistic expression is shown in every field of activity they are engaged in.

## Possible Positive Characteristics

high artistic talent
sense of color
keen appreciation of beauty
imagination
creative thinking

optimism

ambition

gaiety

generosity

loyalty

If Threes take to the culinary arts, they will invariably turn to the decorative and creative aspects of this profession.

## Possible Negative Characteristics

immaturity

irresponsibility

instability

inconsistency

self-centeredness

self-indulgence

fickleness

extravagance

intolerance

self-pity

meticulousness

megalomania

flakiness

overbearing nature

Threes often lack

practicality

pragmatism

long-term planning of their future

Their versatility urges them to take up new challenges before they have attended to matters at hand, and this usually results in the scattering of their talents if they are not well advised and directed, especially in the early stages of their careers. Centralization of purpose and activity is needed on account of their reluctance to harness their talents and use them toward specific ends.

## Behavior in Social Situations

Excellence in speech, including quality of voice, is another outstanding feature of these personalities, which contributes to Threes' forte in public speaking. They are lively and interesting conversationalists and natural entertainers, known for their sense of humor and repartee. As genuine extroverts they can be depended upon to lift the atmosphere of a group or party by their effervescence. However, they are sometimes in danger of talking too much and spoiling much of the good cheer they spread around.

## Financial Outlook

All Threes, whether positive, negative, or in between, are big spenders. Saving money is alien to their nature; they do not feel the need to provide for rainy days and are not depressed when their finances are low. Their sense of values is not focused on the accumulation of money but on the pleasure of using it. Their innate optimism overcomes fear of failure and of the future.

## Career Prospects

Threes are happiest when social, so working in a company where they have lots of interaction with others but also can set their own routine is where they shine most. They are quite capable of doing more than one thing at a time. Though their inherited leadership qualities of the 1 vibration are tempered by the tact and courtesy of the 2, they are usually unhappy in subordinate positions, just as Ones are. They are original and creative, rather than practical and mercenary. They excel in all ceremonial undertakings, whether religious, political, legal, military, or social.

## Romantic Relationships

Whereas the romanticism of the Two personality is of a passive nature, that of the Three is self-initiated and active. They are flirtatious but loyal and delightful companions, with partners who can provide the admiration and affection they need and who can share their variety of interests. They are easily bored and may lose interest in a relationship that does not meet their needs.

Being one of the egocentric trio, Threes concentrate on the joy of living according to their own standards and within their own interests; however, they are capable of remarkable self-sacrifice for a loved one in need of their devotion. Love is the one force that will draw them out of their self-interest. They are not domesticated people and will perform domestic chores only through necessity. Careers and social involvement are far more attractive to them.

## Compatibility

The surest way to get along with these people is to boost their egos. The negative ones see this as a desperate and unconcealed need they have, while the positive ones take it in with subtlety and grace. On the other hand, a certain way to incur their displeasure is to fail to show them the respect they regard as their due.

They have great need for the love and attention of the opposite sex. Negative Threes will perform extraordinary feats in order to draw this attention, but average Threes have no need to do so; their charm, courtesy, and popularity are sufficient. These personalities get on best with Sixes and Nines, and their emotional lives will always be eventful, involving several affairs of the heart. Threes' feelings are easily hurt because they possess the sentimentality and emotionalism of the 2 vibration, though these traits are well concealed behind their extroverted natures.

## Childhood

The high intelligence of Three children may not always be displayed early. Their powerful imagination and lack of practicality keep their minds constantly wandering. They live in a dream world and are often accused of being scatterbrained. This condition, if it exists, is only a passing phase, for these are children with fertile minds who will handle their studies with ease. They grasp facts quickly and don't find it difficult to keep up with their peers. Their vocabulary will develop early and remain above average.

A noticeable trait with these children is their good manners, and this natural courtesy remains throughout their lives. They excel in a variety of sports but will not remain involved in body-contact sports for long. They will always enjoy healthy competition. Most amateur athletes are found in this vibration.

Threes' fierce loyalty to their friends may appear at times to be given at the expense of family loyalty, but this is not actually the case, as these children possess the capacity to handle their obligations to both friends and family. Parents and guardians must accept that children with Three personalities cannot be kept away from frequent social contact, as this is part of their development. A happy family atmosphere with strict guidance is needed to prevent them from wasting their talents.

Threes are not practical and will usually have trouble with timetables and routine duties. Their enthusiasm, imagination, and gift of speech should be constantly encouraged.

## Best Days

The best days for Threes are Sundays, Mondays, and Fridays, especially if these days fall on the 3rd, 12th, 21st, or 30th of any month.

## Style and Colors

These personalities are usually leaders in fashion and may even design their own garments, emphasizing their fondness for bright colors and flamboyant styles. They are attracted to uniforms and do justice to them, as well as to the insignia and decorations that go with them. The colors that blend with their personalities are mauve, violet, purple, blue, crimson, rose, ruby, and amber.

## Stones

Their precious stones are the amethyst and turquoise.

## *Vibration Number 4*

Interaction between the 1, 2, and 3 vibrations produces the stable and earthly 4 vibration. This earthy nature is a result of this number being situated on the physical plane on the numerology grid. The influence of planet Earth stimulates a grounded, pragmatic, and constructive approach to daily life. As the strongest physical vibration, it symbolizes the establishment of a solid foundation for the physical aspects of life. It is a receptive and passive vibration. While the number 1 gives birth to an idea, the 2 gathers facts and figures pertaining to the idea, and the 3 enhances and expands the concept, adding its touch of beauty and artistry, the 4 brings the whole concept down to earth and puts it into form. It is thus the vibration that produces the doer, the worker, and the builder. The mind of the Four personality is focused along constructive lines on the physical plane.

People born on the 4th day of any month are the outright Four personalities. Four personalities born on the 13th, 22nd, and 31st will have qualifying vibrations.

As in the case of other outright personalities from the number 2 onward, the outright Fours will need the number 1 in other areas to help them stay positive. People born on the 22nd have the potential to ascend to the power of this Master Vibration, but here again, they need the assistance of the number 1. Even if they revert to the plain 4 vibration, they will still need the 1. Those born on the 13th and 31st are exceptionally gifted people. They not only have the positive Four attributes but they are also gifted with a powerful imagination as well as aptitude with their hands.

## Distinguishing Traits

pragmatism

trustworthiness

reliability

prudence

loyalty

patriotism

persistence

orderliness

strong concentration

thriftiness

sincerity

dedication to work

proficiency with hands

sensitivity to physical conditions

sound judgment

self-discipline

calmness

good health

conservatism

resistance to lifestyle changes

strong opinions of "right" and "wrong"

traditionalism

The true Doubting Thomas comes from this vibration, especially in regard to abstract ideas and concepts. These personalities demand proof more than the subjects of any other vibration.

Fours have healthy appetites and are able to consume large quantities of food at a time. If a 6 vibration exists in the birthdate as well, these people are likely to have problems with weight, as the 6 vibration usually makes its subjects connoisseurs of food and wine.

## Possible Positive Characteristics

imagination

adaptability

flexibility

ambition

breadth of vision

inspiration

sentimentality

tact

sense of adventure

## Possible Negative Characteristics

inability to cope with emergencies

tenseness

pride

stubbornness

overexactness

fixed opinions

dullness

vulgarity

laziness

passivity

meanness

clumsiness

selfishness

aggression

destructiveness

dogmatism

jealousy

intolerance

greed

dominance

strict disciplinarian

## Behavior in Social Situations

These personalities possess the Twos' capacity to see more than one side of an issue but do not share the Twos' dislike of controversy and argument. On the contrary, Fours have an extraordinary and even aggravating habit of refusing to concede another's point of view, even when they can see its validity. They immediately take up an opposite viewpoint and argue stubbornly. This refusal to concede a point gains them a reputation for being contrary and dogmatic.

Their sense of humor is found in the form of practical jokes and situation comedy. They are mildly extroverted people whose conversation is not necessarily imaginative nor lively but rather confined to practical considerations. They can be deeply hurt if listeners show boredom or condescension on the infrequent occasions they speak out.

## Financial Outlook

Fours constantly seek financial security. They do not gamble but seek to acquire money and material possessions by hard work, sound judgment, and hard bargains. They will not be carried away by impulse or hurried into making a decision. They are thrifty and always have a nest egg set aside. The negative ones can be stingy. This is one of the safest vibrations for the management of money and other financial and property assets.

## Career Prospects

Fours find great contentment when they are making or mending something. They are invariably called upon for help by less practical people and usually give much more than they receive for their labor. Working to excess, with little or no time left for recreation, could be an ever-present problem. Seldom do they show interest in esoteric studies. In their interpretations of life's varied activities, rules, and responsibilities, they are more inclined to follow the letter rather than the spirit of the law.

Fours are drawn into areas of work where dexterity with their hands and bodies can be used to their full advantage. They usually work behind the scenes and are not adventurous in business. They rarely change jobs and interests. The close affinity of the vibration with the earth produces farmers, miners, geologists, surveyors, draftsmen, and workers in any occupation connected with the land. The exactitude that comes with the 4 makes them good accountants, auditors, and economists. They have a keen sense of touch that enables them to produce wonderful physical forms in the world of art, such as sculptures, pottery, carvings, embroideries, and similar creations. They can also excel as masons, surgeons, and healers, or in any activity where the sense of touch is important.

## Romantic Relationships

Display of emotion is not natural to these physically oriented personalities. Displays of affection often embarrass them. They show their love with actions and duty well performed rather than with words and demonstration of emotion; they are not too different from their One counterparts in this regard. As marriage partners, they are loyal but unromantic and austere, and because of this, there is a constant need for others to introduce romance and imagination into their personal lives. Fours can be depended upon to provide a stable and financially secure home, though little or no interest will be taken in beautifying it. They are inclined to exercise stern discipline within the family circle and do this by setting an example.

## Compatibility

Fours need to be dealt with in a precise manner. The surest way to upset them is to indulge in generalizations. Four personalities get on best with other Fours as well as Ones, Twos, and Eights.

## Childhood

Four children are usually healthy, physically strong, and emotionally stable, though undemonstrative. They are soft-spoken and can lack fluency in speech. The negative ones could be stubborn and bullying and may even exhibit a streak of cruelty. These children are not fierce competitors, but their strength of purpose often brings them success over their less determined peers. They excel in body-contact sports.

They can be relied upon from an early age to help around the home and gladly take responsibility for younger members of the family. Their inherent sturdiness provides comfort and strength in the event of a family breakup. It is not in their nature to stray from home. They like to save money, and this tendency will be noticed early in their cautious handling of pocket money.

Their education should be channeled into practical pursuits such as mechanics, technology, engineering, carpentry, or any field that requires aptitude with their hands and the Four's ability to recognize and put into practice the blueprints others provide. Their social involvement will be more in the background of an activity, and they should not be forced into participation in the spotlight if disinclined to do so. Their valuable contribution to society will always be as indispensable workers and helpers behind the scenes.

## Best Days

Sundays, Mondays, and Saturdays, especially if these days fall on the 4th, 13th, 22nd, or 31st of any month, are the best days for Fours.

## Style and Colors

Fours are conservative in their choice of clothes, and the colors they should choose are green, emerald, silver, maroon, and gray.

## Stones

Their jewel is the sapphire.

# *Vibration Number 5*

The vibration number 5 is an outgoing force engaged almost exclusively in gathering as many experiences as possible in life. It is an aggressive and active vibration responsible for expansion and progress, with variety and experience as its chief characteristics. It is also the vibration of the senses, and its subjects possess the capacity to motivate with equal dexterity on the physical, emotional, and mental planes. They also have keen intuition. This is illustrated by the 5's middle position among the 9 digits—four before and four after—and its center position in the numerological grid, which makes it the only number that has communication with all others.

While the 5th day of any month produces the straightforward Five personality, the 14th and 23rd form the complex ones. Those born on the 14th are self-assured and physically oriented and those born on the 23rd are artistic and love movement.

People born on the 15th and 25th, though not Five personalities, are strongly influenced by this number.

## Distinguishing Traits

Fives are not easy to analyze or classify into a particular type due to their restlessness, changeability, and versatility, but some traits are

mercuriality
flamboyance
speed
energy
wit
skill in repartee
enthusiasm
impulsiveness

## Possible Positive Characteristics

adaptability
sociability
resourcefulness
wanderlust
alertness
drive
competitiveness
intelligence
volatility

personal magnetism

curiosity

readiness to plunge into new ventures

quick decision making

bohemianism

unconventionality

## Possible Negative Characteristics

extreme restlessness

uncontrolled activity

desire for change

severe tension

deceitfulness

extravagance

irresponsibility

argumentativeness

self-indulgence

instability

tendency to abuse freedom

caginess

shiftiness

Fives often lack

dependability in routine duties

constancy

self-control

the ability to relax

tolerance of slower personalities

## Behavior in Social Situations

Total absence of oral frustration makes Fives great talkers, and they have an unusual ability to influence and motivate others through the medium of speech. They speak with conviction, though not necessarily with depth of knowledge. When provoked, they can use their power of speech to criticize and hurt. While Three personalities enjoy quality of speech, the Fives possess power of speech, as their delivery is accompanied by emotional expression as well as personal magnetism. Due to their vibrant nature, they find themselves constantly in the limelight.

Fives are extroverted types, but their type of extroversion is focused more on activity and movement than social intercourse. While their personal lives may be disorganized, most of them will try to run and organize the lives of others. They make their own plans and expect others to fall in with them. Governed by the vibration of progress and growth, they are always looking ahead and are found in the forefront of any forward movement. These people have an innate understanding of the need for change, realizing that opportunities for progress are found through new and changing circumstances. More major changes take place in their lives than in the lives of people governed by other vibrations.

## Financial Outlook

Five personalities live for the present and spend money freely. They will not question the price of something or spend time looking for a bargain. They are fond of speculation and gambling and will not avoid a challenge of any sort or fail to take advantage of a get-rich scheme that may come their way. Luckily, those strongly influenced by this vibration enjoy a good measure of success in games of chance.

## Career Prospects

As workers, they are intelligent, energetic, and able to handle more than one task at a time, but they become unsettled in subordinate positions if their freedom of movement is restricted. They are at their best when on the move and in contact with people and when there is some degree of risk and danger in their undertakings. Confinement and routine duties quickly stifle their well-being. This vibration produces the best salespeople, and they also do well in travel and communication. They make good executives and have the ability to stimulate others and keep them constantly alert and enthusiastic. Fives who take to the legal profession will develop expertise in advocacy. They are not given to research work or in-depth studies on account of the urge to move on, and as a result, they gather a variety of knowledge but rarely find time to specialize.

## Romantic Relationships

A quick turnover in relationships may be the fate of most Fives as a result of their desire to keep moving on. Close friendships are rarely maintained, unless it is convenient to do so. They are highly strung personalities and are so alert and quick to react that they have no understanding and tolerance of slow-thinking and slow-moving people. As this is a high-tension vibration, most Fives experience many highs and lows in temperament.

People with Five personalities radiate a sensuous charm with a strong attraction to the opposite sex—an attraction that could extend to several people at the same time. They are more allured by the sensual side of life than those influenced by other vibrations. Their urge for variety in sexual expression places considerable stress upon themselves and their loved ones, who often have to deal with competition. Many of these people will hesitate to marry for fear of surrendering their freedom. On the other hand, many young Fives make hasty and eventually unsuccessful marriages as a result of their impulsiveness and desire for experience.

## Compatibility

The Fives' need for personal freedom is very strong and their partners in any close relationship should make few demands and be free from jealousy and possessiveness. They have no affinity with a particular number or numbers but are able to get along with all types of people; however, they will not hesitate to reject anyone who is unable to keep up with their agile minds and high-powered activity. They will soon end a partnership that has become dull, restricting, and demanding. Their partners will need to assume domestic responsibility, as this vibration is decidedly not a home-oriented one. Tolerance, understanding, and trust will bring out the loyalty of the Five.

## Childhood

Children strongly influenced by this vibration will be physically and emotionally active from an early age. Hyperactivity and tension will be problems with those who express negative qualities of the 5. Their curiosity to explore and experience the world around them will also be displayed early. This strong aspect of the 5 vibration, as well as its impulsiveness, will make many of its younger subjects accident-prone and inclined to a variety of other adventuresome and mischievous actions. They should be trained to look before they leap. They are intelligent, observant, and extremely alert, and are instantly aware of whatever is going on around them. They are strongly competitive and exhibit considerable physical courage when exposed to challenges. Because of their quick reflexes, they make good acrobats, though this could make them somewhat reckless and inclined to take unnecessary risks. They usually excel in all sports, especially those where fast movement is required.

Restlessness will be the major problem. Five children will insist on being heard. Their need for freedom of speech and action will be observed at an early age. Strict control of their education is needed to contain their many natural aptitudes and their tendency to seek many experiences; if not, they will be inclined to switch courses of study too frequently. The jack of all trades and master of none is frequently found here. At home they can be irresponsible, especially with chores and timetables.

## Best Days

Wednesdays and Fridays are the best days for Fives, especially if they fall on a Five day, such as the 5th, 14th, or 23rd.

## Style and Colors

Fives are leaders in fashion and their versatility is also reflected in their attire, which often is not only up-to-date but well in advance of current trends. Their best colors are white, light grays, yellows, and all bright and glistening colors.

## Stones

Their jewel is the diamond set in silver or platinum.

## *Vibration Number 6*

The 6 vibration brings a mental energy into operation, having a tranquil and stable effect on those subject to it. Harmony and balance are its noted features as a result of an equal interaction of physical and spiritual elements. Under these influences, Six personalities seek comfort of the body as well as serenity of mind. This is a receptive vibration ruled by the planet Venus, and people under its influence are extroverted types with evenly balanced personal traits and a loving nature.

Sixes born on the 24th have many similarities to the straightforward Sixes born on the 6th but possess a wider scope for motivation on the emotional, physical, and mental planes. Those born on the 15th day could be difficult to recognize as true Sixes, owing to the influence of two aggressive and adventuresome vibrations in the foreground of their personalities. Essential 6 qualities, however, will remain firm in the background.

### Distinguishing Traits

deliberateness
group-centered
idealism
comprehensive outlook
high sense of civic duty
home stability
variety of social responsibilities
bridge to generation gaps
parental persona
warmth

## Possible Positive Characteristics

responsibility

harmoniousness

congeniality

sympathy

tact

understanding

justness

conscientiousness

peacefulness

unselfishness

diplomacy

dutifulness

loyalty

humanitarianism

hospitality

conservative habits

logical thinking

## Possible Negative Characteristics

worrying

moodiness

subject to depression

overanxiousness

nagging

meddlesomeness

dogmatic opinions

escapists from responsibility

unsympathetic

abnormal jealousy

domestic tyrants

preoccupied with self

fearfulness

intolerance

Sixes often lack

competitive spirit

instant action and reaction

ambition

self-assertiveness

self-discipline

## Behavior in Social Situations

Sixes are pleasant conversationalists and excellent storytellers; all sixes bring entertainment to a fine art. It is easy to enter into an argument with these people, as their logical and analytical minds urge them to question any statement that is not factual. However, they are always fair and good-humored when presenting their points of view. Good food, taken in refined company and elegant surroundings, the fine arts, home entertainment, and simple family life are other pursuits they enjoy. Their love of comfort and ease often exceeds their capacity for adequate physical exercise. When this characteristic is combined with their love of good food and drink, excess weight may be a problem, especially if a 4 vibration also influences the personality. A great deal of organization and planning is brought into their personal and business lives. Domestic discord, dishonesty, vulgarity, and loneliness are most upsetting to their well-being.

## Financial Outlook

In business and home management, Sixes exercise caution in money matters and are very security conscious. They are neither impulsive spenders nor gamblers or speculators. They place their money only in safe investments. In addition, they always manage to balance their budget, but they are inclined to worry unnecessarily about their financial future.

## Career Prospects

Good Six personalities excel in positions of responsibility and trust. They are congenial workers and soon earn the respect of their colleagues. This vibration produces, among other professions, teachers, counselors, social workers, cooks, and businesspeople dealing in home products, food, and accommodation. They are not ruthless or strongly competitive in business. The 6 vibration is also a healing one, and its subjects are attracted to all areas of healing associated with the body and mind. Many excel in community and humanitarian activities.

## Romantic Relationships

Love rules these people, and giving and receiving love is their paramount purpose in life. They are, however, not as physically passionate as subjects of some other numbers, nor are they very demonstrative. Controlled by a mental vibration, reason overshadows their thoughts and actions. Loyalty and devotion to their families are the means by which they display their great capacity for love. Rarely do these people remain single, as the basic need for companionship and homemaking takes priority over other considerations.

Some Sixes, however, remain single if faced with the responsibility of a dependent parent or close relative, but they are still driven by the need to establish a true home setting, regardless of whether it is maintained for the benefit of dependents or a partner and children. Their love of home and their attachment to everything associated with the home and family set them apart from subjects of other vibrations; in fact, this attachment is so strong that the 6 vibration is regarded as the vibration of domesticity.

## Compatibility

Loyalty to their partners is natural. Sixes will not jeopardize the comforts and dignity of home life by indulging in clandestine affairs. Most Sixes have successful marriages. They have a natural flair to choose the right partners and work toward the success of the partnership. However, in some instances, the decision to marry and the choice of a partner is the one occasion where deliberation may give way to haste. Their fundamental need for companionship and a home of their own may override their natural caution. They can also be possessive and overprotective of their loved ones, and are often blind to their faults and inclined to smother them with attention.

## Childhood

Attachment to home is the distinguishing feature of all Six children. They will carry out their share (and more) of domestic chores willingly and without effort. They display an early fondness for cooking. They are not sentimental and cuddly types, though they need and will return a great deal of love and affection. Domestic harmony is as essential to Six children as it is to their Two counterparts; however, they will recover more quickly than the Twos from upheavals in the home and will assume any added responsibility if required to do so.

They are highly intelligent children who are not aggressive, egoistical, or boastful, and who accept personal achievement as a matter of course. They should not be pushed into competition but allowed to choose their own avenues of study and sport. They set their own pace and will retreat within themselves if pressured into action. Gentle persuasion and guidance will always succeed. The logical thinking of this vibration operates from a very early age. A Six child will not be persuaded by arguments not based on reason. Parents can avoid conflict by substituting emotional arguments with thoughtful and reasonable ones.

## Best Day

The best days for important events in Sixes' lives are Tuesdays, Thursdays, and Fridays, especially if they fall on the 6th, 15th, or 24th day of any month.

## Style and Colors

Average Six personalities are not fashion-conscious, and their style and choice of clothing is for comfort and durability. The colors they should use are blue, pink, rose, and orange.

## Stones

Emerald, turquoise, and opal set in gold are the best stones for Sixes.

## *Vibration Number 7*

The spiritual forces outweigh those of the physical in Sevens. Known as the number of God, 7 is the symbol of a vibration representing the mystic element in life. The influence of the mysterious planet Neptune, the planet of Divinity, is seen here.

Concentrated 7 characteristics are only found in those born on the 7th day. In those born on the 16th, the sociability of the 6 vibration and ambition of the 1 obscure many of the recluse tendencies of the 7. People born on the 25th are not easily recognized as Sevens. They may appear extroverted, owing to their love of movement, but many strong 7 qualities remain firmly in the background. This latter group certainly possesses greater scope for variety of expression than those born on the 7th, who are content with intensity of expression. The 17th day and the 27th day also produce personalities powerfully influenced by the 7 vibration. These people may even display more 7 characteristics than those born on the 16th and 25th, since the 7 is in the observable part of those personalities, not the background.

### Distinguishing Traits

objectivity
aloofness
contemplativeness
meditativeness
introspective
skeptical
engage in the abstract
pragmatic
analytical
spiritual self-improvement

seeker of solitude and silence

perfectionism

yearning to live on a higher plane

## Possible Positive Characteristics

poise

personal dignity

mysterious manner

mental courage

self-teacher

empowerment through knowledge

strong intellect

spiritually advanced

## Possible Negative Characteristics

stubbornness

impracticality

rebelliousness

suspiciousness

melancholiness

sarcasm

deceitfulness

intolerance

coldness

relationship leariness

detachedness

self-imposed limitations

introversion

commitment issues

uptightness

reluctance to let go

escapism, often through alcohol

Sevens often need to develop

adaptability

optimism

emotional expression

tolerance

self-appreciation

spontaneity

## Behavior in Social Situations

Sustained sociability in these persons can't be taken for granted; social involvement and popularity are low priorities. They are strongly individualistic and true loners, at perfect ease in their own company. This attitude, unfortunately, makes others feel isolated in the company of strong Sevens. As a result, Sevens are often misunderstood until others realize that they are, in fact, not unsocial but that their need for their own company is greater than their need for the company of others. When the occasions arise, they are able to enjoy company, yet they maintain their detached attitude. They rarely step beyond person-to-person communication. Loved ones apart, this lack of dependence on others for their happiness is a source of considerable power for them.

Sevens are not loud or demanding in their manner but have a quiet way of expressing themselves. They speak only when they have something worthwhile to say, and specialized knowledge is usually evident, along with an unusual ability to reduce complex matters to a few precise words that are pregnant with meaning. This talent is often used to deflate the opinions of pompous people. Sevens show an aversion to frivolous and casual conversation. The constant pursuit of knowledge distinguishes them from others. Most Sevens have an aura of inapproachability, which is another reason why others misunderstand them. Their love of privacy—even secrecy—and unwillingness to explain themselves contribute to this impression. More loners, celibates, and stoics come from this vibration than from any other.

## Financial Outlook

All Sevens have an unusual money sense and are able to develop considerable expertise in handling and investing money. They are not gamblers or speculators but rely largely on specialized knowledge and intuition. Emotion and impulse are not brought into their financial dealings. Their philosophical attitudes also keep them unattached to and independent of their wealth and other material possessions.

## Career Prospects

Seven personalities work best alone. They make excellent research workers and should avoid teamwork and equal partnerships. They need to be free to make their own decisions and can be intolerant of people who do not measure up to their high standards of duty and efficiency. While some of them will be bankers, investors, or higher-education teachers, others will be in forestry, agriculture, farming, water conservation, or anything to do with nature and the land. Still another group may take to science and technology.

It is most unusual to find a Seven personality who is not a keen gardener and environmentalist. They also have a strong attraction toward old things and frequently turn to the study of ancient history, archaeology, paleontology, anthropology, ancient architecture, and ancient music. They like to visit museums, archives, old homes, and gardens, and are attracted to businesses dealing with antiquarian objects.

## Romantic Relationships

As marriage partners and parents, Sevens tend to be possessive. They are loyal and protective and are good providers. They make all major decisions within the family. Marriage is successful when based on mental, cultural, and spiritual compatibility. Though emotionally undemonstrative and embarrassed by sentiment, their love is very deep and constant. Seven personalities make a real effort to preserve the privacy and sanctity of family life.

## Compatibility

Being self-sufficient people, Sevens dislike being fussed over and bothered with details. Talkative and society-loving partners are certain to cause problems. The personal magnetism of these people is known and appreciated only by family members and a few close friends. They are romantic only in the right setting. No personality can turn off as quickly as a Seven if the atmosphere is not conducive to lovemaking.

Sevens seek quiet at home. In a personal relationship, they will not be able to cope with querulous, noisy, and restless partners. Time alone is also essential. They will likely seek partners that are Twos, Sixes, Fours, or Sevens.

## Childhood

Seven children stand out in any family or group on account of their fundamental qualities of detachment and aloofness. Seriousness beyond their years is noticeable. They will show a tendency to avoid group participation and will pass through their school days forming no more than one or two close friendships. They will show great distress if they are forced into a central position in extracurricular activities. They have exceptionally probing minds and are anxious to investigate the nature of things. They have an inclination toward science, technology, and the natural sciences. They are mentally active and do not take kindly to being taught by others; they prefer to be left alone to observe and draw their own conclusions. Parents and guardians must respect these children's need for privacy, for their best development takes place in concentration, contemplation, and seclusion.

They feel a sense of loneliness in their tender years as a result of their shyness, but they are soon able to find companionship and contentment within themselves. Once this discovery is made, they blossom into strong, self-confident children, and their greatest strength will be this newly discovered self-sufficiency. Corporal punishment will be worthless on Sevens. If a subtle mental approach is not used, they will simply withdraw into themselves. They will be good at most sports, though not strongly competitive; winning or losing will be thought of with the innate philosophical attitude of the 7 vibration.

## Best Days

Sundays and Mondays, especially if they fall on the 7th, 16th, or 25th, are the best days for Sevens.

## Style and Colors

Sevens are conservative in dress and should avoid dark colors. Green, white, yellow, and all light shades are best suited for them.

## Stones

Pearls, moonstones, and onyx set in silver are the best stones for Sevens.

# Vibration Number 8

The 8 vibration stands for intense activity in the outer regions of worldly affairs. The 8 is the embodiment of power directed into business, commerce, organizations, administration, and executive authority. The 8 vibration is known as the number of success because of the power it gives its subjects for advancement, achievement, and production. The thought processes of Eight personalities are channeled along constructive lines with constant awareness and concern for future needs.

The strongest Eight personalities are those born on the 8th day of any month, while the 17th and 26th produce Eight personalities with qualified characteristics. Those born on the 17th should take to banking and investment, while those born on the 26th should succeed in businesses relating to accommodations and home products. The 8 vibration has a powerful influence over those born on the 18th and 28th and needs to be taken into serious consideration when these birthdates are examined.

## Distinguishing Traits

deep-seated spirituality
incorruptibility

responsibility

honor

justice

philanthropy

high-minded personality

broad perspective of life

ambitiousness

foresight

practical knowledge

## Possible Positive Characteristics

common sense

deliberation

arbitration skills

tact

authoritativeness

leadership

tenacity

self-assertiveness

self-reliance

strength of purpose

ambition

## Possible Negative Characteristics

irritability

restlessness

aggressiveness

despair

fear

excess of materialism

intolerance

callousness

abnormal desire for personal recognition

Eights often need to develop

artistic imagination

devotion to private study

ability to relax

sense of humor

humility

## Behavior in Social Situations

Those subject to the 8 vibration are extroverted, friendly, and understanding, with sensitivity toward the problems of others. Their emotionalism makes them vulnerable to criticism, interference, and callous remarks. However, they have a fine knack for concealing this vulnerability behind a facade of inscrutability.

Eights make acquaintances with strangers easily, but their busy public lives seldom provide time to turn acquaintances into friendships. They tend to have a few long-term friends, typically drawn from their leisure activities and family connections.

Usually direct and matter-of-fact in speech, Eights are not found among the great talkers. As public speakers, they exude power rather than artistry. They are conservative in all their ways and live strictly within the established order of society.

## Financial Outlook

All Eights have an excellent money sense and are unequaled in financial management of businesses or noncommercial enterprises. This number produces the best business minds, organizers, and executives with a fine knack for delegation. This faculty for choosing the right people for the right tasks is one of the Eights' secrets of success. Considerable deliberation and planning take place before any moves are made. Impartiality is another admirable quality seen in these people, and judgments they hand down on any matter are usually well thought out.

As in the case of Four personalities, reliance is not placed on luck or assistance from others but on steady, hard work. The accumulation of wealth is associated with the acquisition of power; this is what all Eights really aspire to. Those who have succeeded in achieving this goal, however, do not find real fulfillment unless a balance is maintained—on one hand, between power and material possessions and on the other, between ethical, moral, and spiritual values. Their inner spirituality cannot be overlooked, since this forms the bedrock of the 8 vibration.

## Career Prospects

Eight personalities soon find themselves in positions of authority and make splendid superiors. While they can be hard taskmasters who suffer frequent frustration when subordinates do not measure up to their standards of efficiency, they also do not hesitate to show their appreciation for high-quality performance. Their own dedication and enthusiasm make them leaders by example. Restrictions should not be placed on their ambitions, as all Eights possess the potential to rise well above the average in professional or business fields.

Many eminent professional athletes and coaches are found here. They are courageous, determined, and enduring competitors. They have a strong tendency to become totally involved in their work, into which they put a great deal of emotional effort. The need for relaxation in areas other than regular work is often overlooked.

## Romantic Relationships

In personal relationships, Eights are tactful and gentle, but at the same time, they are firm and authoritative if necessary. They can be identified by their unconscious directing and managing of the people around them.

Eights are excellent providers who take great pride in their families. They are also loving and greatly in need of love, but all too frequently, they do not find time for romance, sentiment, and personal involvement with family affairs. The authority they are accustomed to in public life is too often exercised in the domestic scene.

## Compatibility

Partners of Eights in marriage, or any personal relationship, give more of their labor and affection than they receive, because Eights tend to involve themselves in the business side of their lives at the expense of home, loved ones, and social responsibilities. Their partners need to prod them to meet their social obligations. Their homes are seldom open for entertainment and, if given their own way, are kept strictly as a family domain. Eights' apparent unsociability is unintentional, resulting from their intense dedication to their profession. They need the precious little time they allow themselves for enjoyment of their families. They are best with Twos or Sixes.

## Childhood

The feelings of Eight children are easily hurt until emotion is brought under control with maturity. Their behavior is often tinged with aggression, as they will take some time to understand the power that lies within. This aggression will be exhibited to a greater degree if there is also a strong 1 vibration in the birthdate.

Eights' capacity to take control and assume the role of leader will be revealed early, especially if an emergency arises. Their innate sense of justice makes them strong supporters of the underdog. Some friction is bound to follow when they meet up with other Eight personalities. While being encouraged to participate in all kinds of sport, their education should be carried to the university level, for these children are not meant to occupy subordinate and unskilled positions in life. The subjects they choose for study should be those that will lead them into business, administration, and the law. High ambition should be encouraged. Eights are serious-minded children. This is not a domesticated number, and Eight children may not willingly participate in their share of home duties but will be found to be neat and orderly in their personal habits.

## Best Days

For events in Eights' lives, Sundays, Mondays, and Saturdays, especially if they fall on the 8th, 17th, and 26th day of any month, are the most beneficial.

## Style and Colors

Eight personalities choose clothing of the best quality and they pay careful attention to detail. Their best colors are dark gray, black, dark blue, purple, and brown. Light shades should be avoided.

## Stones

The precious stones Eights should wear are amethysts, black pearls, black diamonds, lapis lazuli, and other dark-colored stones.

## *Vibration Number 9*

As the highest of all primary or single-digit numbers, 9 is known principally as the vibration of wisdom and stands for a high state of mental and spiritual advancement. It is, in fact, an all-embracing vibration that signifies completion. It contains the initiative of the 1, the gentleness and grace of the 2, the imagination and self-expression of the 3, the sense of proportion of the 4, the alertness and progress of the 5, the responsibility of the 6, the desire for perfection of the 7, the discernment of the 8, and, as a natural progression, wisdom, compassion, and universality of its own.

As a far-reaching and impersonal vibration, the 9 does not confine its subjects to self, family, community, or country. The 1 gives individuality, the 9 universality.

While unqualified Nine personalities are found among those born on the 9th day of any month, those born on the 18th day are disguised by the strength of the businesslike 1 and 8 vibrations. These people are capable of considerable achievement, since they are backed by the internationalism of the underlying 9. The 27th also produces outstanding Nines with greater leanings toward uncompetitive pursuits and the study of the inner side of life.

### Distinguishing Traits

selflessness
broad-minded humanitarianism
cosmopolitan lifestyle
worldly outlook
understanding
forgiveness
honor
honesty

charm

generosity

## Possible Positive Characteristics

attraction to power and fame

enjoyment in sharing wisdom

extrasensory perception

generosity

global outlook

humanitarianism

idealism

insight into identifying mental or
    physical illness

intuition

love of inquiry into the mystical

love of meditative pleasures

personal magnetism

practicality in expression

restorative power

sensitivity to atmosphere, color, and sound

spiritual and psychic gifts

wisdom

## Possible Negative Characteristics

bitterness

irritability

abnormal fear of having feelings hurt

defensiveness

aggressiveness

closed-mindedness

fanatical religious beliefs

unstable emotions

egocentricity

oppressiveness

extreme secretiveness

inflexibility

aimless dreaming

critical of others

unprepared to give love

selfishness

self-love

superiority

indecision

procrastination

lack of concentration

impracticality

lack of commercial sense

impressionability

## Behavior in Social Situations

The depth of wisdom in the 9 vibration places great pressure on Nines to control their emotions whenever they meet with narrowness, bigotry, and parochialism. The stronger ones are able to contain themselves and even express compassion; the weaker ones often lose control and resort to outbursts of anger and biting sarcasm.

## Financial Outlook

Nines display generosity, which they are noted for in the handling of their finances. The average Nine is regarded as a soft touch. The basic compassion of the 9 vibration, combined with impressionability and indifference toward accumulation of material wealth, contribute to this situation.

## Career Prospects

These personalities function best as professionals. They lack business acumen because of their generosity and disinterest in commercial competition. They are best suited to a wide contact with all types of people, especially in areas where the 9 quality of human understanding can be used. If these personalities happen to be involved in mundane work that inhibits their imagination and resources, it is advisable that they find hobbies in the fields of art and literature as outlets for their cultural talents. Many Nines who are not able to reach the full extent of their potential in their professions find satisfactory personal outlets in charitable works, involvement in relief, welfare, and refugee organizations, or similar humanitarian activity within the established churches.

They travel because of their wide interests in human culture. They gather a great deal of knowledge, particularly in the fine arts. The cultural aspects of life become as important to the developed Nines as the spiritual and humanitarian sides. Many strong Nines, however, run the risk of gathering a considerable store of learning and then losing touch with its practical application.

## Romantic Relationships

As marriage partners, positive Nines are broad-minded, sympathetic, tolerant, and free in giving. Their spouses, unless of a similar bent, may often find it hard to cope with their generosity and breadth of vision. Nines can also keep emotional grudges to themselves until they become overwhelming and explode in virulent, critical outbursts.

## Compatibility

Problems are bound to arise with narrow-minded and materialistic partners. Nines are usually attracted to people who measure up to their standards of idealism and refinement. They are passionate and devoted with the right partners and always give more than they receive. They are not domesticated, however, and personal freedom is needed for their many outside activities.

## Childhood

Most precocious children are Nines. Their opinions frequently amaze their elders, who wonder how and where such knowledge was acquired. The innate wisdom of the 9 vibration reveals itself as soon as these children are able to speak. From an early age, they should be guided away from self-centeredness, narrow-mindedness, and extreme forms of nationalism. Their early conflict between selfishness and the establishment of an unselfish lifestyle will become evident by sudden changes in moods, from tolerance and extreme generosity to coldness, withdrawal, and self-interest. Nines are liable to change swiftly from a state of great happiness to one of anger and disillusionment. They are deeply emotional but unable to demonstrate their emotions except in sudden outbursts of temper, when their minds can no longer contain conflicting sentiments. They find much joy in contemplative and meditative pleasures. As refined, courteous, and nonaggressive children, they will not be fierce competitors. This will not hinder them, since their intelligence and natural talents will usually make them winners.

## Best Days

For Nines, Tuesdays, Thursdays, and Fridays, especially if these days fall on the 9th, 18th, or 27th day of any month, are the best.

## Style and Colors

An international touch is seen in Nines' choice of clothes. The colors that suit them best are red, carmine, lavender, olive, pink, wine, and rose. They should avoid black.

## Stones

The best stones for Nines are ruby, garnet, bloodstones, and other red-colored stones.

# The Master Vibrations: Numbers 11 and 22

Beyond the 9 vibration, there are two others of higher frequency symbolized by the unreduced numbers 11 and 22. Known as Master Numbers, they may be found in any of the six Spheres of Influence and will affect the life of that person according to the nature of the particular Sphere of Influence in which they are found. These are intense and powerful vibrations, and the majority of people who possess them find it difficult to live continuously within their high frequencies. Only a few advanced individuals are able to remain permanently on these high vibratory levels. When not living up to the demands of these Master Vibrations, these people revert to the influence of the base numbers 2 and 4, respectively.

## *Vibration Number 11*

The 11 vibration shares many characteristics with the 9, particularly the surrender of personal ambition for spiritual and cultural interests. It is essentially the vibration of spirit, and those influenced by it are not commercial in outlook. Being an intensified vibration, it makes great demands upon the personality, especially if it is found in the Sphere of Destiny. The two 1s of the 11 contribute positivity and willpower, adding considerable strength to the underlying 2, which is not found in a straightforward 2 vibration.

### Distinguishing Traits

inspiration

vision

intuition

spirituality

evangelism

zeal

gift of prophecy

revelation

### Possible Positive Characteristics

passionate reformer

active imagination

idealism

visionariness

innovativeness

forward thinking

forerunner of the new Aquarian age

## Possible Negative Characteristics

dogmatism
fanaticism
superiority
impracticality
indecisiveness
aimlessness
eccentricity
hypocritical practices
self-infatuated
disconnect with human relationships

## Behavior in Social Situations

The average Eleven personality finds it hard to resist the urge to expound firm opinions to all and sundry. In turn, they are frequently misunderstood and subjected to ridicule by more earthbound people.

## Financial Outlook

Due to their unmaterialistic outlook, Elevens have little desire to hold on to their possessions and are therefore spontaneous givers. They would rather give than receive. As they are motivated by the vibration of spirit, they are able to drive themselves to greater lengths than most others, and as the spirit never tires, they do not consider retirement from their activities.

## Career Prospects

These people also take to science and excel in space-age scientific inventions. They possess to a greater degree the inventive genius of the straightforward One personalities. Their inventions, however, are not confined to scientific interests and can range from designing clothes and domestic products to improving living conditions. Idealism, rather than commercialism, is behind the Elevens' urge to invent. They are also found to be psychologists, astronomers, astrologers, and mediums. Their keenness to explore the inner being is assisted by strong intuition and psychic ability. Their need for artistic expression is equally strong. They often become

powerful orators
evangelists
missionaries
reformers
philosophers

## Romantic Relationships

As partners in marriage, Elevens are not easy to cope with unless their spouses are on the same wavelength. Their advanced ideas and unconventional lifestyle sometimes place a strain on the domestic scene. Their partners should not be materialistic or parochial in their desires and attitudes. The Elevens will not show patience, tolerance, or understanding if there is incompatibility in a partnership. Many Elevens tend to lose personal direction, bringing disorder into their lives and the lives of those close to them.

## Childhood

Eleven children possess the wisdom and insight of their Master Vibration in latency. Attentive parents will observe gradual development of the Eleven's attributes. A quick intake of knowledge will be an early indication, as will be an early attraction to music.

> *NOTE: For best days, style, colors, and stones, those of the 2 vibration apply. Only two types of Elevens are found in the First Sphere of Influence: the straightforward Elevens, born on the 11th, and the complex personalities, born on the 29th. A great deal of emotion takes control of those born on the 29th.*

## *Vibration Number 22*

While the 11 vibration brings out the spiritual messenger, the 22 produces the spiritual builder, combining both spirit and matter. The vibratory power of the 11 is doubled in the 22, giving it not only greater intensity in the spiritual realms but also the balancing trait of practicality. It contains the attributes of every other vibration in a well-balanced combination of the spiritual and practical. This combination gives the 22 a consolidated power not found in any of the other numbers.

The 22 vibration may appear in any of the six Spheres of Influence but will be most influential in the first and second as the personality type or as destiny. Positive Twenty-twos are found only when the number 1 is present in the birthdate, such as 1/22/1966. A birthdate that will be vulnerable to negative expressions is 5/22/1958 = 32 = 5, due to its excess of emotion, created by the 5 in the birthday and destiny. Another that is susceptible to negative expression is 2/22/1924 = 22, due to its abundance of Twos. The willpower of the 1 vibration is needed in order to handle this Master Vibration.

## Distinguishing Traits

The practicality of the basic 4 of this Master Vibration works in harmony with the spirituality of the 22, making its subjects practical visionaries and idealists operating on a horizon that is wider and more comprehensive than the 9 or the 11. While sharing the same international outlook as the Nines and Elevens, the Twenty-twos have the potential to fulfill their ideas, dreams, visions, and projects.

## Possible Positive Characteristics

wisdom

quick learner

practical knowledge applications

well-balanced emotions

unconventional lifestyle

late bloomers

Twenty-twos sometimes have difficulty coming to terms with their higher spiritual natures and the many practical responsibilities in the material aspects of their lives. This conflict is overcome once they develop a sense of objectivity and no longer associate their personal feelings with the many activities they become involved in.

## Possible Negative Characteristics

personal-gain pursuits

materialism

obsession with wealth and power

loneliness

self-centeredness

inferiority complexes

ruthlessness in bids for power

## Financial Outlook

Twenty-twos of all ages are good money managers.

## Career Prospects

An advanced academic education will be of great advantage to these individuals so that there will be no outside hindrance to their using the unlimited potential they possess. This unlimited potential leaves all avenues open.

## Romantic Relationships

Twenty-twos, whether positive or negative, cannot be tied down to domesticity. However, their capacity to play a dual role as good providers and protectors of home and family, as well as being public figures, is recognized and appreciated by their partners. Twenty-twos demand freedom and resent interference, dominance, and any restrictions on their movements.

## Childhood

Twenty-two children display dexterity early. They function as good Four personalities until maturity opens their thoughts to wider perspectives. Most Twenty-two children will keep a little piggy bank.

*NOTE: Twenty-twos' best days for business activity, style, colors, and stones are the same as those for the 4 vibration. Only one Twenty-two personality type—those born on the 22nd day of any month—appears in the First Sphere of Influence.*

## The Cipher 0

While the 0 does not represent special characteristics, it does serve to intensify the features of a number it is attached to and, in turn, the personality as a whole. The position of the 0 in the birthdate has to be taken into consideration when determining the extent of its effect on the personality. It could be in a position with no appreciable influence on the personality. Its strongest effect is felt by those born on the 10th, 20th, or 30th of any month. The birthdays 19th and 28th also contain 0s in a concealed position, since both numbers reduce to 10, giving added strength to the 1 vibration.

In the birth month (only the 10th month), the 0's power to influence the personality is diminished considerably—so much so that it may be considered ineffective. In the birth year, where the vibratory influence of the numbers is the weakest, it has no power at all.

Limitations are placed on personalities with an abundance of 0s in their birthdates. The more 0s present, the fewer the avenues available for expression. The following are some examples of how a 0 can or cannot influence a personality:

**5/10/1976:** Without a 0, this birthdate would produce a self-confident and positive personality, but the presence of the 0 increases the strength of the 1 vibration, giving it even greater chances of success.

**11/10/1911:** The 0 here is not advantageous, since it merely increases the strength of an already rigid personality, owing to an excess of the 1 vibration.

**8/30/1963:** This birthdate, even without the 0, is inclined toward the negative aspects of the 8 vibration. The presence of the 1 vibration in the birth month would have alleviated this situation.

> *NOTE: The 1 vibration in the day of birth or in the month always ensures positivity.*

**2/20/1982:** Possible negatives of a Two personality are increased by the repetition of the 2; the 0 then amplifies this.

**3/3/1980:** The 0 does not do anything to increase the negativity of a Three personality that may already display some negatives—due to the 3 occupying the birth day and month—since it occupies the weakest position in the birthdate.

**6/18/2002:** This is a strong and well-balanced birthdate. The most the 0s would do is enhance certain features.

# 3

---

# THE SECOND SPHERE OF INFLUENCE: SPHERE OF DESTINY

## The Birthdate Totaled

The next number that possesses a strong, independent function is the single digit arrived at by adding the numbers of the birthdate. This forms the Second Sphere of Influence. For example, the birthdate 6/17/1927 is simply added across, as follows:

$$6/17/1927 \quad 6+1+7+1+9+2+7 = 33 \quad \longrightarrow \quad 3+3 = 6$$

The Second Sphere of Influence for this birthdate will be governed by the 6 vibration. The Master Vibrations 11 and 22 (see page 2) are not reduced to 2 and 4, respectively, when they are the end total but remain as 11 and 22, as the following examples illustrate:

$$11/13/1976 \quad 1+1+1+3+1+9+7+6 = 29 \quad \longrightarrow \quad 2+9 = 11$$
$$10/10/1964 \quad 1+0+1+0+1+9+6+4 = 22$$

This number holds the combined force of all the numbers of the birthdate, thus giving it considerable power and high regard among numerologists as the sphere that discloses the purpose behind an individual's existence. It is known by many names, such as the Destiny Number, the Life Path Number, the Number of Fate, the Ruling Number, the Birth Force Number, and the Life's Lesson Number. All these names, while giving a clear description, carry essentially the same meaning. The most popular ones, however, are the Destiny Number and the Life Path Number.

Seen as the Destiny Number, or the Number of Fate, this sphere indicates the reason and purpose of our birth and shows the directions in which we should guide our development and the type of work we are best equipped to undertake. As our Ruling Number or Birth Force Number, it indicates the type of power or energy we have been endowed with and that is to be used throughout our life. As the Life's Lesson Number, it points out the lessons we have come into this life to learn, adjustments to be made, and personal qualities to be acquired.

To summarize, the Destiny Number, or the Second Sphere of Influence, indicates what qualities we should recognize, acquire, and adapt to and what vocations and hobbies we should choose. To aid us in doing so, there is a natural pull or push, as the case may be, in the direction of this vibration's characteristics. Personality traits found in the First Sphere of Influence that complement the possibilities of the Second Sphere will naturally make life smoother, whereas such traits that conflict with the Destiny Number would suggest some difficulties, adjustments, and challenges.

People who are aware of their Destiny Number and its call and who consciously steer themselves in its direction should find greater fulfillment in life. This is the number given to someone who asks what his or her number is. The Destiny Number is often found associated in some way with the many events in our lives. It frequently turns up in dates of important personal events, in names of close relatives, places, and even in material possessions such as house numbers, car numbers, important personal documents, and sums of money. To this extent at least, it will be seen that the Destiny

Number, as its name implies, has an influence on our lives. This number should be consciously used for important events and other activities.

When the Destiny Number does not show up, other numbers that are in harmony with it will. These can also be used in lieu of or in addition to the Destiny Number. The following is a list of numbers that are in harmony with each other. They may be used or regarded as alternatives, not only in this sphere of destiny but in other areas as well.

Number 1   3, 5, 7
Number 2   4, 8
Number 3   1, 5, 6, 9
Number 4   2, 8
Number 5   1, 3, 7
Number 6   3, 9
Number 7   1, 3, 5
Number 8   2, 4
Number 9   3, 6

The analysis on the following pages reveals the major purpose of our lives according to our Destiny Number. Many of the points should be familiar to us, but if they are not, there is a great deal of unfulfilled potential in our lives that could bring us happiness and satisfaction.

Young people especially, or those analyzing the destiny of a child, are in a position to choose the direction that can yield the greatest rewards. People are not placed on earth to forever blunder and stumble without direction or purpose. Numerologists and adherents of various schools of philosophy and religions believe that we are here so we can learn particular lessons and achieve recognizable aims. These lessons are directly linked to the unique personality traits and destiny offered to us by the numbers of our birthdate and name.

The influence of the month and year on the personality type should be given serious attention before a final assessment of the personality is made. Then it is important to observe their influence on the destiny vibration. The numbers of the birth month and year have a direct influence on the personality type and an indirect influence on the Destiny. It is the complete personality that is responsible for fulfilling the requirements of Destiny.

As we gain moral and spiritual understanding of our identity and our lives, we develop as human beings and contribute to the evolution of society. The degree and direction of destiny fulfillment depends upon the strength of the personality type (shown in the First Sphere of Influence). This important fact, which applies to all the Destiny Numbers, must be kept in mind.

## *Vibration Number 1 as Destiny*

As individuality is the hallmark of this vibration, a course of individual thought and action is called for. Subjects of this Life Path will want to strive for independence, with the conviction that their future lies in their own hands. Success will be achieved by following the development of such qualities as

self-confidence
self-sufficiency
self-reliance
ability to overcome obstacles
willpower
self-control
courage
originality
initiative

creativity

leadership

Ones will want to avoid

dependence

expectation of support from others

These people may leave home early and lead independent lives, but family loyalty will remain strong. Friendships will be restricted to a few old and trusted companions.

It's important to note that a 1 destiny does not automatically indicate a leader. The alternative is the individualist or loner who will avoid both subordinate and authoritative roles in life and remain just their own person. The forces of this vibration will push those with this destiny to act in a manner in which they will remove themselves from restricting, subordinate, and subservient positions. This is not the destiny of the follower or the collaborator.

This destiny's principal motivating force is the desire for personal advancement, and those with it will want to place self before others. Whether care will be taken to do so without hurting or causing injustice will depend on other Spheres of Influence. The subjects of this destiny should realize that a cooperative spirit can be acquired without losing their individuality.

People favored by this destiny will be unconventional and frequently break away and set their own patterns of behavior. They will not tolerate interference and criticism. Their originality and creativity will be confined to the physical plane.

If a 1 destiny is combined with a personality that is susceptible to negative aspects, especially a One, Four, or Eight personality, the subjects with a destiny will tend to be dictatorial, egotistical, overconfident, selfish, hypersensitive, boastful, and set in their ways. The birthdate 4/4/1964 = 28 = 10 = 1 is an example of a 1 destiny.

## *Vibration Number 2 as Destiny*

The 2 destiny is the direct opposite of the 1. While people with a 1 destiny may turn out to be leaders, loners, or masters of their own lives, people with a 2 destiny are inclined to enter into associations, fraternities, and partnerships. They will want to take a supportive role and enjoy communal living. Also, while egoism is the chief trait of the 1, the 2 destiny makes no demands for a display of ego. Success will be achieved by developing and embracing the following:

self sufficiency

diplomacy

mediation

negotiation

peacemaking

inner composure

willpower

decision making

the power of silence

the value of the spoken word

The "king makers" of politics or the "powers behind the throne" are usually those with 2 destinies. To elaborate on this facet of the 2 vibration, let us take a glimpse into the inner meaning of numbers. The 2 vibration, as mentioned earlier, is the primary receptive force with a negative polarity. The word "negative" is used in its electrical sense, meaning "force that does not act but draws to itself and retains power through magnetic attraction." The 2 vibration is really a reserve force or storehouse of power.

Essentially, the 2 Life Path is one of giving rather than receiving, particularly the giving of self in service to others. Twos will want to do this willingly, and in return, they will receive ample reward in accordance with the law of compensation and the law of attraction.

They will be drawn toward group activity where they can display adaptability, agreeability, and friendliness. The principal motivating force behind their destiny is the need to establish tranquility in their surroundings. Following the path of marriage, companionship, and association, a lonely life is not the lot of those with this destiny. They cannot and will not remain single. Social problems will be nonexistent unless the personality type as shown in the First Sphere of Influence is overly sensitive and therefore easily hurt.

A 2 destiny combined with a Two personality tends to lean toward the negative. For instance, 2/2/1960 = 20 = 2 is likely to involve the individual in several emotional affairs accompanied by heartache and failure. A desperate need for security and companionship may drive such a personality into a hasty and ill-advised marriage. Psychosomatic illnesses may also cause problems, resulting in a dreary personality.

## *Vibration Number 3 as Destiny*

The 3 destiny, with its vibrations of freshness and vigor, leads its subjects into the lighter and brighter sides of life, giving them a constant urge for self-expression in these areas. As versatility is one of the distinguishing features of this vibration, self-expression can take several forms. Success will be achieved by

inspiring and motivating people
embracing their love of beauty, color, and music
cultivating a wide range of friends

With Threes being essentially happy and optimistic extroverts, social involvement should be a high priority in their lives. Endowed with the gift of entertainment and a genuine sense of humor, they will seek to hold the center of attention in order to find fulfillment. Their best expression will be through the spoken word, while singing, acting, and writing will also be avenues of expression.

Occupations and hobbies chosen will—and should—invariably be those that will allow Threes' artistic talents to be displayed. New and unconventional ideas will often bring them into conflict with the established order of society. This is not a destiny that will seek comfort and security in a quiet domestic scene. Domestic responsibilities should not be allowed to hold these people back, as their strongest need will always be self-expression on as wide a scale as possible, which is the essence of the 3 vibration.

Combined with a personality that has limited expression, making it prone to negative expression, this destiny will also produce negative qualities, such as self-absorption, criticism, intolerance, and strong escapist tendencies. There will also be a powerful need for constant emotional attention from others without a similar response from the Threes themselves. The birthdate 3/3/1977 = 30 = 3 is an example of such a destiny.

## Vibration Number 4 as Destiny

Whereas the energies of the 3 are concentrated on the mental and artistic realms of life, those of the 4 will be firmly directed toward establishing a solid foundation on the physical side of life with a practical and commonsense approach. The field of activity of the Fours will not be wide, adventuresome, and colorful, but will be concentrated on a few projects requiring physical work and practical application. Emphasis will be placed on material acquisitions with a sound sense of values guiding Fours' decisions. Money might be spent judiciously, and an appreciable amount will always be set aside for the future. The gambler will not be found with this destiny. Fours will develop early in life and will want to continue to cultivate

responsibility
duty

loyalty
dependability
community service

Others make many demands on the time and energy of those with this destiny, and Fours' talents are put to constant use. Governed in this sphere by the vibration that produces the builders of social order and upholders of tradition, they soon become known as the solid citizens of their community.

This is a stay-put vibration, and herein lies its strength. Those with a 4 destiny will not want to change direction once on a chosen course. Travel is not part of this destiny, as Fours usually find themselves too busy to indulge in this pastime. They may be subject to becoming too absorbed in work and should be advised to seek periods of relaxation. A sense of humor and imagination are not strong qualities of this vibration and attempts should be made to develop these qualities.

Those with this destiny and a personality that tends toward the negative have the potential of being dull and dreary, and will possibly fall into a rut and be content to remain there. They can be extremely reluctant to part with their money and possessions and can find themselves in a situation where they do not possess their wealth but their wealth possesses them. The birthdate 6/6/1963 = 31 = 4 is such an example.

## *Vibration Number 5 as Destiny*

Freedom is the watchword of this destiny and those subject to it should—and will—strive to acquire freedom of thought, speech, and action and to learn the responsible use of these. They may expect change, variety, and travel in their lives. Adaptability and flexibility will be required of them to cope with the many unexpected changes that will take place. This is destiny that can achieve growth and advancement through adaptation

willingness to let go of the old

powerful speech development

discipline

attention to detail

Fives regard life as an adventure to be experienced with enthusiasm and energy. They live each day with a greater degree of intensity than those with other Life Paths. Due to the comprehensive nature of their outlook they are soon able to feel at home wherever they are and adapt to all types of people and customs.

Young people with this destiny vibration can become sullen and uncooperative if restricted and will rebel against authority. Freedom fighters, whether religious, political, social, or otherwise, are most often subjects of this destiny. Proficiency in foreign languages is more easily acquired by this vibration than by others.

This destiny gives its subjects the opportunity to express a wide variety of talent, but some negative qualities such as restlessness, impulsiveness, self-indulgence, and the tendency to speak out without enough knowledge should be brought under control.

Combined with a personality that is susceptible to the negative, especially a negative Five, such as 5/5/1984 = 32 = 5, misuse of freedom can become a real danger, plus indulgence in sensuality, drink, drugs, and gambling.

## Vibration Number 6 as Destiny

People with this destiny should steer their lives in the direction of the general qualities of the 6 vibration. It is known as the path of responsibility, particularly in the domestic, social, and humanitarian fields. On one hand, there is a strong pull toward these responsibilities; on the other, most of these people will need to prepare themselves to assume such responsibilities by making changes in their personal attitudes and lifestyle. They will want to

be aware of this need to make personal adjustments
learn not to look for perfection
learn to adjust to and accept circumstances and people as they find them
seek to establish harmony, comfort, and beauty in the domestic scene

The well-developed artistic appreciation of this vibration is reflected in the furnishings of their homes. They may also become connoisseurs of wine, food, and art. Having secured domestic felicity and personal balance, they will turn their attention to community needs, especially as counselors, teachers, guides, and peacemakers.

They will rarely tend toward the critical, and those who have fully set themselves on this path of humanitarian service should strive to submerge their own egos in order to build up the deflated and bruised egos of others. Love of the physical and spiritual aspects of life will operate with equal force. It is this characteristic that makes those with this destiny accessible and credible counselors to people of all ages. More than others, Sixes are able to teach the meaning of love and understanding, which they invariably do by example.

A negatively expressed personality with this destiny is likely to be domineering, unreasonable, possessive, and jealous, especially in regard to domestic issues. A constant urge to whine, nag, and find faults will make life difficult for their partners. Someone with a birthdate such as 6/2/1960 = 24 = 6 may be subject to this type of negativity.

## Vibration Number 7 as Destiny

This is a Life Path where the mind should be used to transfer interests from the material and physical realms to the abstract and subtle. It does not, however, indicate that those subject to it should cease to engage in the affairs of the world. They should work to

look upon all material possessions with detachment
pursue their quest into the eternal truths of life
not permit worldly possessions to enslave them
constantly examine their motives and maintain only enduring values
not acquire superficial standards
overcome the urge to withhold their knowledge from others
be more outgoing
establish harmony and self-appreciate to counterbalance perfectionism

An infinite capacity to gather abstract knowledge awaits those who take up the challenge of this destiny. Their worldly activities will always be tinged with the wisdom they will acquire, and their philosophical attitude will help them overcome the disappointments and changes of life.

Those with a Seven destiny should chose a profession in a specialized field that will use the vibration's power to investigate and analyze. Their best work is carried out alone, or with very few fellow workers around, away from crowds, noise, and commercial activity. They will be better suited to become professionals than to enter the business world. However, those engaged in business enterprises will and should strive to work to be high principled and honest and will not indulge in unscrupulous competition.

Personalities that are more likely to express negativity and who have this destiny are certain to seek seclusion and various forms of escapism from social and other mundane responsibilities. Birthdates such as 7/7/1973 = 34 = 7 and 2/2/1992 = 25 = 7 are examples.

## *Vibration Number 8 as Destiny*

The wide world of commerce, industry, government, organizations, and corporations are the fields of activity open to those with this destiny. It is by no means a domesticated or parochial Life Path, nor is it one for dreamers and visionaries. Their energies should be directed toward success in the practical, managerial, and financial affairs of life.

To succeed, Eights will want to cultivate their natural tendency for

courage
ambition
dedication
motivating themselves and others
social and economic justice
benevolence

Unless a balance is struck between their responsibilities and obligations, the law of cause and effect will neutralize the success gained and fulfillment of this destiny will not be achieved. These people must be wary of the trap of materialism and power for power's sake.

Needless to say, not all Eights will reach the top of their chosen vocations, but their destiny indicates that they should strive to do so; the result will be advancement well beyond the average. Their field of endeavor could, for instance, range from management of a single supermarket to the management of a multinational company. Promotion will be automatic when their enthusiasm for work, practicality, and energy are displayed and observed.

Most with an Eight destiny will find themselves acting as counselors in financial and economic affairs. As many people will look to them for guidance, they will need to remember the responsibilities thrust upon them by their positions of knowledge and authority. Unless supported by emotional numbers in the birthdate, people with this destiny will have problems with emotional expression. Although compassionate and sympathetic, they will resent having to express these sentiments, especially if they happen to stand in the way of their public life. All with this destiny should be conscious of their dress and general appearance as an important aspect of their public image.

When in a personality that tends toward negatives, especially a negative Four or Eight (for example, 8/4/1994 = 35 = 8), those with this destiny can express both mental and physical cruelty from time to time.

## *Vibration Number 9 as Destiny*

This is a difficult destiny to follow, and the extent of success achieved will depend largely on the personality type. As this is not a destiny for quiet suburban or country living, strong Nine personalities combined with the 9 destiny find the 9 influences greatly magnified, and when confined to this type of life, Nines will suffer much frustration and unhappiness. Freedom of movement will be sought, not only for humanitarian activity but also for cultural advancement. Artistic talents could be carried to high levels of achievement. Keen spiritual awareness will find these people involved in metaphysics, mysticism, and studies in comparative religions. The fulfillment of the 9 destiny calls for

self-adjustment
the surrender of the personal for the impersonal
sublimating self-centeredness for the welfare of humanity
rising above the prejudices of race, class, and religion
acceptance of the worthiness of the humanitarian Life Path

The Brotherhood of Man should be the principal concern of these people. All forms of separatism that contribute to social and economic injustice and that hinder cultural intermingling should be avoided.

As this is by no means a domesticated Life Path, partners should allow these personalities considerable freedom of movement and reconcile themselves to the fact that the love of Nines will reach out well beyond home, family, and community. They will place no importance on material security and their energies will not be spent in this direction.

Those with personalities that tend to express the negatives of the vibration and who also have a 9 destiny, such as those born on 9/9/1935 = 36 = 9 or 6/6/1995 = 36 = 9, are likely to be egocentric, moody, fickle, critical, and ill-tempered. They will display a feeling of bitterness toward the world and project a facade of wisdom and knowledge they do not possess.

## Vibration Number 11 as Destiny

Birthdates totaling 29 and 38 have this Master Vibration as a potential destiny. People who do not take up this path will follow the destiny of the straightforward 2 vibration. However, for those who follow the 11 destiny, there is unlimited potential for personal advancement in metaphysical studies and the development of clairvoyance, intuition, and prophecy. It is not a destiny that calls for the pursuit of personal gain in terms of material wealth and power; it calls for the spiritual side of life to be awakened. Once this awakening takes place, these people should learn the practical application of their spiritual gifts.

Those with the 11 destiny will want to enter areas of activity that will not only facilitate spiritual growth but also provide scope for the application of their higher values. The inventive genius of the 11 vibration will have wide opportunities in both the arts and sciences. Down-to-earth and practical associates will be of invaluable support to Elevens, for such associates will bring about a fine balance between vision and inspiration on one hand and common sense and pragmatism on the other. These associates will also be able to place some restraint on the spontaneous generosity that is a staple of this destiny.

## *Vibration Number 22 as Destiny*

This is the most powerful of all the destiny vibrations, giving its subjects unlimited resources for expansion as master planners and builders in all departments of human activity, especially those who leave behind lasting benefits for the welfare of mankind. Not many individuals with this Life Path are able to lift themselves to the peak of its vibratory power and meet its challenges, but the few who do will become world renowned. The average person with a 22 destiny who avails themselves of the power of this Master Vibration will invariably make a name for themselves in their chosen fields of activity.

This is a multitalented vibration containing the features of all others, and those whose destiny is the number 22 may choose any field of endeavor and meet with success. Politics, business, the professions, government service, and large humanitarian organizations are all open. Twenty-twos who are oblivious to the nature and power of their destiny will revert to the standard 4 destiny.

# The Birth Month and the Birth Year

To complete the analysis of the influences of the birthdate, we will examine the numbers of the month and year of birth and their bearing on the personality as a whole.

## *The Birth Month*

The number or numbers of the birth month are not as strong as those of the birthday, nor do they possess an independent function or create personal identity as the numbers of the birthday and the Destiny Number do. They work in conjunction with the other numbers of the birthdate and influence them to act in either a favorable or unfavorable manner on the personality. They may provide an essential vibration, giving balance to the personality, or overload a personality with an already strong vibration. The 9th month, for instance, will contribute negative influences on a birthdate such as 9/9/1935 = 36 = 9, and favorable influences on a birthdate such as 9/4/1941 = 28 = 10 = 1. In the first example, a straightforward Nine personality is stifled by too many 9 characteristics, resulting in a lack of balance and avenues of expression, causing negative traits to enter the personality. In the second example, the comprehensive 9 vibration opens up a staid Four personality.

Like the birthday, the birth month may have a single-digit or a multiple number. The 11th and 12th months are not reduced to a single 2 and a single 3 but in the 11th month are considered two 1s and as a single 1 and a single 2 for the 12th month. The zero of the 10th month may be disregarded, since it does not have an appreciable influence on the personality from this position.

Further examples of the influence of the number or numbers of the birth month are as follows:

$$5/2/1955 \quad 5+2+1+9+5+5 = 27 \quad \longrightarrow \quad 2+7 = 9$$

The 5 vibration of the 5th month overloads the emotional aspects of a sentimental Two personality. Emotion has too strong a hold on this personality and can hinder the responsibilities of the 9 destiny.

$$1/2/1955 \quad 1+2+1+9+5+5 = 23 \quad \longrightarrow \quad 2+3 = 5$$

The 1 vibration of the 1st month is strong enough to control emotionalism and give self-assurance to the Two personality and will also assist in coping with the 5 destiny.

*11/29/1969  1+1+2+9+1+9+6+9 = 38*  ⟶  *3+8 = 11*

The two 1s of the eleventh month add strength to an already strong birthday. There will be no problems in fulfilling an 11 destiny.

*8/12/1933  8+1+2+1+9+3+3 = 27*  ⟶  *2+7 = 9*

The 8 vibration of the 8th month draws the Three personality out of self-centeredness and helps with the wide-ranging 9 destiny.

*12/3/1992  1+2+3+1+9+9+2 = 27*  ⟶  *2+7 = 9*

The 1 of the 12th month gives positivity to the Three personality, and the 2 vibration extends the range of the artistic and social attributes.

*3/22/2001  3+2+2+2+0+0+1 = 10*  ⟶  *1+0 = 1*

This is an outstanding example of a Master Vibration controlling a positive personality. Positivity is gained through the 3 in the birth month.

## The Birth Year

The numbers of the year of birth provide additional vibrations but do not have as strong an influence on the personality as the numbers of the birth month do. They do, however, provide outlets for expression and thereby bring balance to the personality as a whole if they are not found in either the birthday or birth month. They may also contribute to an overload of vibrations, as in the case of someone born on 3/3/1933.

The numbers of the birth year are of a supportive and influential nature only and do not possess an independent function.

When analyzing the variety of influences within a birthdate, we need to recognize the relative importance of the numbers' positions and the fact that when the same number appears, it has a weakening effect over the personality, leading to negative attitudes. This weakening takes place when the repetition of a number is found in the stronger areas of the birthdate, such as the birth day and birth month. In the birthdate 3/3/1933 given in the previous paragraph, the two 3s in the birth year have merely aggravated a birthdate already prone to the negative. The 3s would not have overwhelmed the personality if the birthdate was 12/3/1933. In this case, the numbers of the birth month give balance to the Three personality and the two 3s of the birth year are not strong enough to override the power of the numbers of the birth month. Two more examples illustrating the influence of the numbers of the birth year are

$$4/24/1944 \quad 4+2+4+1+9+4+4 = 28 \quad \longrightarrow \quad 2+8 = 10 \quad \longrightarrow \quad 1+0 = 1$$

The 4 vibration is strong here. Although this is a Six personality, many 4 influences control the individual and are prone to negative expression. If these influences can be checked, the positive 4 qualities will help with the 1 destiny.

$$4/21/1944 \quad 4+2+1+1+9+4+4 = 25 \quad \longrightarrow \quad 2+5 = 7$$

The 1, 2, and 3 vibrations control this personality with the help of the 4 in the birth month. The two 4s in the birth year will contribute but not in a negative way, since the 4 in the birth month does not control the personality.

# 4

## THE THIRD SPHERE OF INFLUENCE: SPHERE OF THE GIVEN NAME

The vibrations of the name contribute to the Third, Fourth, Fifth, and Sixth Spheres of Influence. The given name is the Third Sphere of Influence and can play a significant role in balancing the vibrations of the First and Second Spheres. If areas of conflict appear in the birthdate, the vibration of the Third Sphere can neutralize the conflict, but it can also intensify the problem. People can use given names in a way that enhances the birthdate and creates more balanced individuals who will be better prepared to fulfill their potential.

While the given name has the most important role in a name, the vibrations of the middle name or names (if any) and the surname all add to the composite of a personality. The surname reflects hereditary tendencies and family resemblances. Hence by sharing the same surname, members of the same family also share the same numerological influence. The total of the numbers in their surname gives them a common bond. The middle name or names are passive and do not have an independent function but contribute to the formation of the full name and the number of the full name. This contribution could be valuable when the given name and surname are both short, such as Ann Hill or Ian Hall. The letters, and numbers, of these names are so few that the supply of vibrations to the overall personality is low.

Without supporting vibrations from the name, a strong and balanced birthdate is needed to succeed. When the numbers of the name are listed and compared with the birthdate numbers, the advantage of having at least one middle name will become apparent. More information on this aspect of the complete chart is given in chapter 9.

"What's in a name?" is a question we hear from time to time. Shakespeare asked this question and added that "a rose by any other name would smell as sweet." While a rose may smell as sweet when called something else, there is a great deal of significance in a name, and the giving of any name that is constantly used is indeed a matter worth serious consideration.

The given name may be our parents' decision or our own. Often a middle name or some other name unrelated to those on the birth certificate may be in use. It is this name that identifies, gives individuality, and has the most significant effect on the personality. For instance, a child with the name of Michael John Edwards may sooner or later be addressed as Mike or Mick. Or he may choose his middle name, John, which may be turned into Jack. If these changes take place, his abbreviated or changed name will become the Third Sphere of Influence.

When a given name is chosen, it's important to take into consideration the common practice of multisyllabic names being abbreviated or altered. If a new version is used permanently, it will be the name that holds the power. For example, if the name Genevieve is chosen for its 4 vibration, the girl may lose it to the 11, formed by Genny, or the 5, from Jenny. Similarly, James may become Jim (5), Jimmy (7), or Jamie (2). There is something to be said for parents insisting that children are called by the name they know is best.

Some people may always be referred to or addressed by their initials, shortened names, or titles, or by double or even triple names. Some examples are J. R. R. Tolkien,

Boss, Chief, Oscar Wilde, and Ralph Waldo Emerson. There are others who have two sets of names, one used in business and another by family and friends. In the case of initials and double or triple names, the total of the initials or the total of the multiple names is the number to consider. For people who use two sets of names, the vibrations produced by both names are equally important and should be examined to see whether they are in harmony with the particular area of activity they are influencing. Nicknames and pet names possess the same power and influence as the given name. People who have these extra names will have two or more vibrations influencing them.

A name is, in fact, a sound. The human body is a finely tuned instrument with keen responses to all sorts of extraneous vibrations, particularly sound vibrations. There is an instant feeling of well-being when a sympathetic vibration is encountered and one of displeasure with an inharmonious vibration. As all bodies have different rates of vibration, they do not respond in the same way that others do to a certain vibration, whether sound or otherwise. Herein lies the importance of a given name that is in harmony with a particular type of body and personality. An inharmonious name will be like a discordant musical note causing discomfort, restriction, and imbalance. This point is well illustrated by William Congreve:

> *Musick hath Charms to soothe a savage Breast,*
> *To soften Rocks, or bend a knotted Oak.*
> *I've read that things inanimate have mov'd,*
> *And, as with living Souls, have been inform'd*
> *By Magick numbers and persuasive Sound.*

The classical name Jason has been in vogue in recent times. The vibration of this name is 5, and it would be a splendid name for a male born on 3/11/1991 = 25 = 7. The vital connecting link of the 5 vibration will balance well within the personality. This name, however, will not be suitable for a boy born on 5/5/2002 = 14 = 5, for example. Hyperactivity and excess of emotion, among other difficulties, will be the result of overloading the 5 vibration.

Care should therefore be taken to choose a given name that fits with the First and Second Spheres, either giving balance to the personality in an area that has none or adding to an area that has a number but needs strengthening.

Whenever possible, preference should be given to 1 or 5 names, for these are the true activators. In a well-distributed birthdate, such as 6/23/1964 = 31 = 4, a 1 name is most advantageous because it gives strength and self-confidence to a multi-talented personality. The number 1 in the century of the full date does not produce these qualities due to its weak placement.

If a birthdate is found to be strong as well as balanced and no help is needed from the given name, the best choice will be a name that is in harmony with the Destiny Number. The question of overloading does not arise, since the Spheres of Influence are different. A birthdate such as 3/18/1981 = 31 = 4 does not need help from the given name to strengthen the personality, but a 4 name will be best so that added help is given toward fulfilling the 4 destiny.

However, the given name influences the personality and therefore shares common ground with the First Sphere of Influence, which forms the personality. The vibrations of the given name should not clash with, weaken, or disturb the vibrations of the First Sphere of Influence. For instance, a birthdate such as 8/8/1983 should not have an 8 name, and a 3 name would be most unsuitable for someone born on 3/3/1983.

Parents choose names for their children from many sources. Names of family members are often repeated in the next generation, names are borrowed from well-known personalities, popular names spread rapidly, or parents can express their creativity with a unique name or unusual spelling. While these names may please the parents, the children are not always grateful, and in fact may feel handicapped.

Names that are obviously dated at the time of naming can be an embarrassment to the children and they may also create the wrong vibrations. The same can be said of names for famous or popular heroes and heroines in novels, much admired sports-persons, movie stars, or other celebrities. The practice of naming a baby for purely sentimental reasons can and should be avoided; any concerned parent can choose a name from among hundreds that will be in harmony with the birthdate. In doing so, they will make a significant contribution toward the development of a well-balanced individual. The idea is that the name should not only be pleasing to the parents but also one that will relate favorably to the personality and destiny of the child.

The final choice of the name should be made after many alternatives have been examined, not only for their direct influence on the personality but also for their very significant contribution to the formation of the three other Spheres of Influence, especially the number of the full name. It is important for parents to remain flexible about a name for their baby. They should consider each name carefully and concentrate on the name that sounds best or feels right.

Numerologists believe that parents are not the only ones who have an effect on the choice of their child's name; higher forces also influence the decision. Though parents may systematically analyze the factors described in this book and narrow down the list of prospective names, they should also try to let intuition play a part.

## *Changing the Given Name*

As adults, we already have a name and need to work with it to produce harmony within the personality and a lifestyle that is successful. A complete change of name is necessary only in special circumstances. An adult should first try changing the spelling of their name if a change is considered necessary.

It may sound far-fetched, but it has been proven that a change of name will, in most instances, slowly but surely cause a corresponding change in the personality or amplify certain characteristics of the personality. Sometimes the change is quite sud-den. The length of time it takes to notice a change will no doubt depend on the purpose of the change and the numerological potential to respond to the new vibration. Generally, an instant change should not be expected.

The vibrations of the new name will take time to influence the personality, depending on the degree of identification the person has with the new vibration. This process might take three months or three years, depending on the individual.

Existing potential is essential before a new name can trigger a change of career or cause a career to escalate. If a name is changed for this purpose, as in the case of many artists, actors, and people entering religious orders, the vibration of the new name should not only harmonize with the Second Sphere of Influence (Destiny) and the Fourth Sphere of Influence (Expression of Talents) but also with the particular career chosen. In other words, the sound of the new name must be pleasant and appropriate to the career intended. Innumerable actors who have found their original names a liability have achieved success by adopting pleasant sounding names of compatible vibrations.

Changing names to suit vocations, especially in religious orders, has been a common practice for centuries. Both the Old and New Testaments of the Bible are replete with instances of names being deliberately changed before a specific vocation or mission. Many people also change their names for the sole purpose of bringing about balance and harmony within the personality.

Although the idea of changing one's name may sound attractive at times, it is not a step to be taken without serious consideration and consultation if necessary. Many questions should be asked and answered before a decision is made, such as

Is a change really necessary?

Have the Birth and Name Grids been examined properly? (This is discussed in the next chapter.)

What are the motives for the change? Are they for frivolous or escapist reasons? (Often it is better to retain the name and overcome any obstacles, real or imagined, that it may cause.)

Has advice been sought and considered?

Has a change of spelling of the present name been considered? (This is often the best alternative. The same pronunciation can be retained by adding, removing, or changing a letter or letters. The change in spelling of the name alters its rate of vibration and correspondingly the influence upon the personality. One should seek the most suitable vibration, not merely a new name that happens to be currently popular.)

If any doubts linger after these questions have been considered, a numerologist's opinion should be sought. The final choice of a name, however, always rests with the parents or the individual. A third party should only give an opinion.

# 5

---

# THE NUMEROLOGICAL GRID

The previous chapters, in which the First, Second, and Third Spheres of Influence were discussed, have largely illustrated the characteristics of the numbers as an independent function. However, as indicated in the previous chapter in particular, they are defined more specifically by their relationship with the other numbers. It is this interaction, while creating positive, negative, and neutralizing influences, that contributes to forming the complete personality and affecting destiny.

In this chapter, our aim is to develop an understanding of how the First and Second Spheres of Influence operate simultaneously and what happens when the given name is then introduced. In order to do so, it is necessary to study in detail the interrelation of numbers in the birthdate. This is best done by first examining the influence each number of the birthdate has on the vibratory structure of the personality and then considering the nature of the Destiny Number. Having studied the characteristics of both spheres separately, our next step will be to look at them together, as two interconnected parts of the composite personality.

The easiest way to illustrate the First and Second Spheres of Influence is through the use of a simple numerological grid. A complete grid with all the single numbers in their permanent positions is shown below, to the left. When considering the grid, you should also keep in mind the more detailed classifications for each number, as shown in the chart on the right.

## FIXED GRID

| | | | |
|---|---|---|---|
| *3* | *6* | *9* | **Mental Plane** |
| *2* | *5* | *8* | **Emotional Plane** |
| *1* | *4* | *7* | **Physical Plane** |

Self    Community    Global

**(Consciousness)**

| | |
|---|---|
| Number 1 | Physical/Mental |
| Number 2 | Emotional/Intuitional |
| Number 3 | Mental/Emotional |
| Number 4 | Physical |
| Number 5 | Emotional/Physical/ Mental/Intuitional |
| Number 6 | Mental |
| Number 7 | Physical/Intuitional |
| Number 8 | Emotional/Mental |
| Number 9 | Mental/Intuitional/ Emotional |

The zero, lacking qualities of its own, may be placed for convenience's sake with the 1. Needless to say, no birthdate will fill all the squares of the grid.

The three horizontal planes are levels of expression. This is, however, a general classification, since most vibrations share some common characteristics, though they may express them differently. (The vertical planes of consciousness are discussed further on page 114.)

The numbers of one plane are not more desirable than or superior to another. These planes indicate methods of expression—the impulses that reveal not only thought and feeling but also personality traits and tendencies. Above all, they indicate the area or areas where the greatest amount of power is concentrated. This can be seen at a glance once the numbers of a birthdate are correctly placed within the grid.

The areas of power form the individual's personality type. When this is figured out, the first important comparison can be made and the relationship between the First and Second Spheres of Influence becomes evident. For example, if the power base of the First Sphere is on the physical plane and the Second Sphere is as well, one should not meet with many difficulties in establishing a successful lifestyle. On the other hand, if the First Sphere is on the emotional plane and the Second is on the physical plane, there is bound to be some inner conflict when fulfilling the requirements of destiny.

Mind governs the mental plane. Everything is carefully considered before action and reaction. People on the emotional plane refer all things to their emotions; the heart governs the personality. Those governed by the physical plane have their thought processes geared toward the body and practical, earthly undertakings. A down-to-earth form of thinking governs these people, and those with intuitional vibrations will learn to trust their instincts and premonitions.

Spirituality is a power that is spread throughout all vibrations. Each number channels the spiritual through the personality according to its qualities. For example, some personalities fulfill their spirituality through worship, others through service, and still others through concentration and meditation.

Having few numbers on the mental plane does not indicate that the individual has no mental capacity; it merely shows that the mind is directed toward emotional or physical pursuits, where high intelligence and initiative may be displayed.

Similarly, the absence of emotional plane numbers does not mean that emotion is lacking; the outlets for display and demonstration of emotional qualities simply may not be available. Such personalities may appear to have greater control over their feelings, though they could be seething inside. They may resort to defensive or evasive behavior in order to cope with their difficulty in naturally expressing their feelings. This usually results in restriction of intimate expression, leading to misunderstanding by others. Body contact in the form of spontaneous embraces, hugs, and other forms of endearment will be distasteful to their nature. These people will undoubtedly be loving, yet they may seem incapable of expressing their love.

Those individuals with only the number 1 from the century of the full date on the physical plane will most likely have no interest or aptitude in the physical side of life, unless support is given through the Fourth Sphere of Influence, where the appropriate talents are found. The mind is generally used instead on the mental or emotional levels, or both, according to the birthdate.

Thought processes of individuals with vibrations predominantly confined to one plane will act according to the qualities of that plane. On the other hand, individuals with mixed numbers will have little difficulty in functioning confidently and naturally on any two or more of these planes.

Finally, the 5 vibration, although a strongly emotional one, is nevertheless the only vibration that gives expression on all three planes, plus the intuitional level. A number 5 in the birthday or birth month has a stabilizing influence on the personality as a whole because of its multiplicity of expression. A 5 name will be most helpful to someone with an excess of numbers on either the mental or physical plane, or for one with no numbers on the emotional plane.

Vibrations form themselves into three other categories, which in turn place people into three fundamental types. This can be seen in the vertical lines of the grid. Numbers 1, 2, and 3 represent vibrations of individuality, and people under their influence are oriented toward self and self-interests. The pronouns I, me, and mine figure largely in their thoughts, speech, and actions. The "me first" attitude is a common feature of these personalities. Objective consideration of issues may be foreign to their nature.

The principal characteristic displayed by the thoughts of the Ones is originality; the Twos, fantasy; and the Threes, creative imagination

The vibratory influences of the numbers 4, 5, and 6 represent community consciousness. They are numbers of action. The thought processes of subjects of these numbers project out of self and into the community. The down-to-earth labor of the Fours, the intense nervous energy of the Fives, and the constant mental activity of the Sixes are further distinguishing features.

The numbers 7, 8, and 9 denote power and widespread influence, giving their subjects an orientation toward international consciousness. This power is found in the spiritual depth of the Sevens, the authority and justice of the Eights, and the humanitarianism of the Nines.

## Examining the Grid

Once a grid picture has been constructed by placing the numbers of a given birthdate in their correct positions, and the First and Second Spheres of Influence are highlighted, preliminary work on the personality may begin.

### *Planes of Expression*

Look for the area or areas of power in the planes of expression. An evenly distributed set of numbers will indicate an ability to motivate on two or more planes. Numbers with the base of power confined to one plane will indicate whether the individual is essentially physically, emotionally, or mentally oriented. However, secondary characteristics may be revealed by numbers on other planes. A mentally oriented person, for instance, may possess secondary characteristics on the emotional plane, as in the case of a birthdate such as 9/12/1980 = 30 = 3. A lopsided set of numbers with heavy overloading on any one plane or the repetition of a single number can result in a closed-in or negative personality, or it can produce genius (though the former is more common than the latter).

## Consciousness on the Grid

Next, observe the vertical squares in their order. Consciousness of self is emphasized in the area covered by the 1, 2, and 3 vibrations, while community consciousness is added to the 4, 5, and 6 vibrations. A global awareness is characteristic of the 7, 8, and 9 vibrations. Here again, balanced or one-sided personalities can be seen.

## Blanks in the Grid

Note the absence of a number in the squares of a particular plane. This important point indicates that the individual under examination has no outlets for self-expression on that plane. At the same time, it is also advisable to note all other blanks in the grid because these reveal that the birthdate has not supplied the individual with the qualities particular to the missing vibration.

The blanks in both the horizontal and vertical sections should be carefully noted as well, not only as areas revealing lack of power and expression but also as areas that should be concentrated on when the Spheres of Influence for names are examined. The whole name often provides balancing vibrations. However, if no help is available from the names, these blank areas will remain as weaknesses that may need to be developed as well as possible throughout life.

## Positivity and Negativity

Once the power base and weak areas have been established, the next important factor that can be recorded is the degree of positivity or negativity that exists within the personality.

The determining factor will be the presence or absence of the 1 vibration. Willpower, self-assurance, and self-control, which are the outstanding qualities of the 1 vibration, should be looked for, since it is principally these qualities that contribute to determining a positive personality or a negative one. However, it is advisable to suspend final judgment until the four Spheres of Influence of the whole name have been examined.

## The Second Sphere in the Grid

The Second Sphere of Influence, or the Destiny Number, should be considered on its own in the first instance. Once the attractions, directions, and lessons indicated by this sphere have been established, it should be reconsidered in relation to the First Sphere, the personality type. In regard to vocations and other activities in life, the directions of an individual's destiny points should be noted first. Next, the lessons to be learned and the qualities of character to be acquired should be observed. Finally, one may take the essential step of observing whether the personality type and supporting numbers help fulfill what the Destiny Number requires—in short, whether the First Sphere of Influence complements the Second Sphere or whether there is conflict. An easy life or a personal battle will be indicated by the answers.

## Active and Receptive Vibrations

There are active vibrations that represent expenditure of energy and there are receptive vibrations that represent the storage of energy. The odd numbers are active and the even numbers are receptive. It is always very interesting to observe which numbers predominate. The odd numbers are also inspirational and freedom-loving, whereas the evens are practical and home-loving. For instance, a female with active odd numbers predominating will be an ambitious career person with strong leadership and creative tendencies.

The grid can also be an easy reference to particular characteristics of the personality being analyzed. The points that follow are a quick guide to some of many significant personality traits that can be seen. (These are covered in more detail in chapters 2 and 3.)

## Extroversion

The grid pattern shows whether or not an individual under examination is an extrovert. Almost all vibrations, whether on the positive or negative side, favor this facet of the human personality. For instance, a Two personality is an extrovert who enjoys group activity but prefers to remain in the background. Three and Five personalities are also extroverts, but they demand the center of attention. The Seven personality, being a quiet, contemplative type, will display this trait in small, well-controlled doses.

Once again, the presence or absence of the 1 vibration will influence the degree and quality of extroversion. Natural introverts may be produced by the 1 vibration or the 7, and these people could be adopting a positive form of introversion where they just prefer their own company to the company of others.

## Competitiveness

The competitive spirit is found among the odd numbers. The 1, 3, and 5 vibrations make strong competitors, while those influenced by the 7 and 9 are only mildly interested in competition. The even numbers are not competitive, with the exception of the 8, which falls firmly into the strongly competitive category.

The ability to pick the presence or absence of a competitive spirit in a particular area of activity is a grave responsibility held by parents and guardians. They should examine this quality in a child before forcing or influencing them into an area of activity where strong competition is needed.

## Domesticity

Numerology clearly shows that it is the vibratory makeup alone, and not the sex, that divides individuals into career people, domesticated ones, and the many that are in between. The even numbers produce the home-oriented ones, while the odd numbers create the outgoing ones not given to domesticity and a quiet family life. People with birthdates such as 11/2/1998 = 31 = 4 or 4/16/2002 = 15 = 6, whether male or female, will be more inclined to embrace domestic duties rather than follow a career in public life.

## Oral Expression

Oral expression is seen in many interesting forms, depending on the First Sphere of Influence. Generally speaking, the Three and Five personalities are the impulsive talkers. The taciturn ones are the Ones and Sevens, while the genuine conversationalists are the Sixes, Nines, and Twenty-twos. The authoritative ones are the Ones, Fives, and Eights. The shy ones who speak only when they are addressed are the Twos, while the quiet ones who speak only when they have something worthwhile to say are the Fours. The Ones and Sevens also fall into this last group and are at ease when they speak on their specialty. The Elevens enjoy giving their points of view to all and sundry. A Five will be ready to speak about any subject, regardless of any specialized knowledge, and the temporary enthusiasm they display may soon be lost once the subject is closed. The argumentative ones are found among the Sixes, who are also the best storytellers. Ones, Fours, Sevens, and Eights are forthright and brief in speech, and people who possess an abundance of these vibrations can be curt and peremptory.

## A Note on Environment

So far, personal characteristics and potential have been examined, but no consideration has been given to heredity and environmental conditioning. There is no doubt that these factors enhance, obscure, inhibit, and generally influence, for good or ill, our individuality. The growing psyche of the child is shaped and molded by his or her family, community, and nation, according to the customs and norms prevailing at the time of the child's growth. We can hardly escape this conditioning, but fortunately, with the growth of the personality, we often outgrow it, allowing our true selves to blossom. There may be some, however, who fail to do so because fear, ignorance of self, or lethargy may have taken over. These unfortunate people may live their lives unaware of their multifaceted potential. Therefore, whenever something of a person's background is known, we should try to determine the degree of individuality and the degree of submission to this conditioning.

# Negativity

Negative tendencies arise when a positive force is not present in the full birthdate. For example, 1900 birthdates are without a 1 anywhere and so are considered negative, whereas 1901 birthdates gain a positive. Negative tendencies are also found in 1972 and 2009 birthdates if there is no 1 in the day or month or when there is a repetition of the birthday number in the birth month. These tendencies may arise in active or passive forms. The vibratory force that ensures a positive disposition is the 1 vibration. For this reason, it is known as the Activator. (The number 1 present in the birth year of all persons born in the 20th century is in a weak position and does not exercise much influence on the personality formed by the birthday and supported by the birth month.)

Individuals suffering from negative features due to the absence of 1 in their birth day or month far exceed those with a repetition of their birthday number. The latter condition can happen only with single-digit birthdays. Personalities found in the former condition normally possess an even distribution of numbers or vibrations and, consequently, multiple talents and avenues for self-expression. However, as the driving force of the number 1 is not present, they are likely to underestimate and undersell themselves. They often show surprise and disbelief when their potential and capabilities are pointed out to them. Some typical birthdates of people with these problems are 6/23/1984 = 33 = 6, 9/27/1984 = 40 = 4, and 3/5/1984 = 30 = 3. Insufficient self-confidence and self-assurance can always be overcome with a careful upbringing, education, and self-realization. These individuals are likely to be pleasant and likable, as they do not possess the disagreeable traits of egotism, self-promotion, competition, and pride. Any harm they do will be to themselves and not to others, and such damage will be the result of omission rather than commission.

This form of negativity can be checked by the choice of a first or given name that vibrates to the number 1. With its constant and powerful influence, it is bound to give the required lift to the personality. The urge to forge ahead will constantly be experienced. The 1 vibration appearing in the Fourth Sphere of Influence (the whole name), the Fifth Sphere of Influence (vowels), and the Sixth Sphere of Influence (consonants) will also be of considerable assistance.

In the case of a single-digit birthday, repetition of the birthday number in the birth month creates an overloading of the qualities of their birth force. This results in a weakening and, in some instances, a strengthening in negative ways of these qualities. The individual is confined to a narrow world of thought and action. Here again there could be some relief if their first name opens up fresh channels.

This second form of negativity can also be helped by the vibrations of one or more of the four Spheres of Influence within the names. However, the mitigating power will not be as strong as in the first type, owing to the concentration and closing in of negative traits when a single vibration is found in more than one sphere. Some help can also be obtained from a whole name, which gives a good all-around balance of numbers that the birthdate lacks, as in the following example:

$$4/4/1940 \quad 4 + 4 + 1 + 9 + 4 + 0 = 22$$

$$CAROLINE \quad JAYNE \quad MACINTOSH$$
$$31963955 \quad 11755 \quad 413952618$$

Number of times vibrations appear in the whole name:

| Vibration | Quantity of Letters |
|:---:|:---:|
| 1 | 5 |
| 2 | 1 |
| 3 | 3 |
| 4 | 1 |
| 5 | 5 |
| 6 | 2 |
| 7 | 1 |
| 8 | 1 |
| 9 | 3 |

Our example shows that there are five letters with the 1 vibration, one letter with the 2 vibration, and so on, up to the 9 vibration. When these vibrations are placed in the grid, their influence in relation to the birthdate can be interpreted easily.

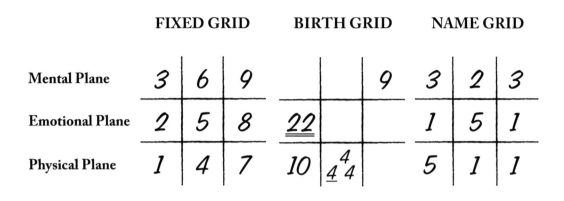

|  | FIXED GRID | | | BIRTH GRID | | | NAME GRID | | |
|---|---|---|---|---|---|---|---|---|---|
| **Mental Plane** | 3 | 6 | 9 | | | 9 | 3 | 2 | 3 |
| **Emotional Plane** | 2 | 5 | 8 | <u>22</u> | | | 1 | 5 | 1 |
| **Physical Plane** | 1 | 4 | 7 | 10 | <u>4</u> 4 <sup>4</sup> | | 5 | 1 | 1 |

The mental plane, which is blank in the birthdate, except for the 9 in the century of the birth year, has been greatly strengthened. The emotional plane has been helped by the 5 vibration. Positivity has been introduced by the 1 vibration on the physical plane.

Most importantly, the name Caroline vibrates to the number 5, which alleviates the drabness of the 4 personality.

More information on this part of our analysis is given in chapter 9. The analysis of the numbers of the birthdate is now complete. These first two Spheres of Influence have the strongest bearing on the formation and development of our personalities.

We are fortunate if all or most of the vibrations of our birthdate combine in harmony and we can find direction easily. However, if the vibrational influences are in conflict, the challenge we face is how best to manage the divergent influences pushing us in different directions. In many cases, self-discipline and sheer willpower can contain the effect of contrary and negative tendencies. But other personalities may need some assistance. This assistance may be provided by the name. If the name is ineffective or emphasizes weaknesses rather than giving strength and balance, it may be beneficial to modify the name to produce positive influences.

**4/23/1967 = 32 = 5**

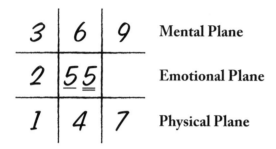

*Note:* *The First Sphere of Influence is underlined once. The Second Sphere of Influence is underlined twice.*

**Comments:** This individual is multitalented and well-balanced but lacking in drive as a result of the absence of a strong 1 vibration. A 1 name is essential for self-confidence.

**5/31/1972 = 28 = 10 = 1**

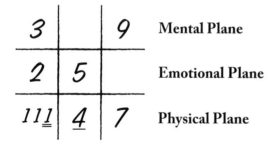

**Comments:** This person is strong, well-balanced, and multitalented. Assistance from the name is not called for, but a 6 name, giving domesticity, would be good.

**4/1/1940 = 19 = 10 = 1**

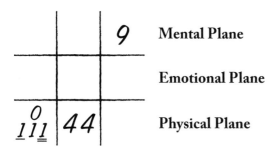

Mental Plane

Emotional Plane

Physical Plane

**Comments:** This is a physically oriented person, and a 5 name should be chosen for flexibility, imagination, and oral and emotional expression. Names with physical plane numbers would increase rigidity and should be avoided.

**2/20/1958 = 27 = 9**

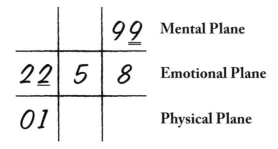

Mental Plane

Emotional Plane

Physical Plane

**Comments:** This individual is emotionally overbalanced. A 1 name is essential to reduce emotionalism and provide some stability in the physical plane. A 4 or 7 name would be good second choices. Names with emotional plane numbers should not be considered.

**9/3/1935 = 30 = 3**

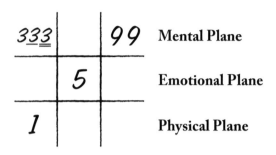

Mental Plane

Emotional Plane

Physical Plane

**Comments:** This birthdate creates a mentally overbalanced individual. A 4 name would be best to bring this personality down to earth. Good alternatives would be 1 and 7 names. Names with mental plane numbers would threaten mental stability.

**1/12/1931 = 18 = 9**

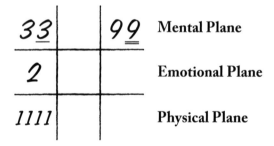

Mental Plane

Emotional Plane

Physical Plane

**Comments:** This person is a bit egocentric. A 5 name would help the personality cross over central blanks and help fulfill the wide-ranging 9 destiny. Names that should be avoided are 1 and 3 names.

**7/7/1977 = 38 = 11**

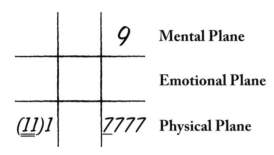

| | | 9 | **Mental Plane** |
| | | | **Emotional Plane** |
| (11)1 | | 7777 | **Physical Plane** |

**Comments:** This person would be introverted and pedantic, but a 5 name would open up the personality. A 2 or a 3 name would be good alternatives and would soften rigid attitudes. A 7 name would be disastrous.

**1/5/1988 = 32 = 5**

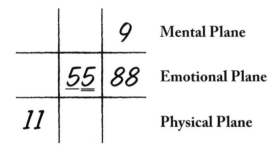

| | | 9 | **Mental Plane** |
| | 55 | 88 | **Emotional Plane** |
| 11 | | | **Physical Plane** |

**Comments:** As the 5 vibration controls both the First and Second Spheres of Influence, excess of speed and excessive expenditure of nervous energy could be a problem for this person. A 4, 6, or 7 name would slow down the personality. A 5 name would cause excessive tension and hyperactivity.

**2/21/1997 = 31 = 4**

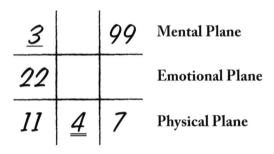

**Comments:** This birthday creates a versatile personality with positive attitudes. A 6 or 4 name would assist destiny and add a link to the second vertical area of the grid. A 5 name would bring in too much emotion.

**5/5/2000 = 12 = 3**

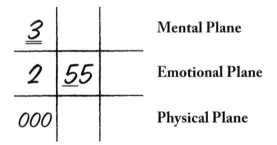

**Comments:** Extreme restlessness and instability will be shown by this negative Five personality with a Three destiny. A name with another mental or emotional number would aggravate these problems. A name with a physical plane number is essential.

**2/7/2002 = 13 = 4**

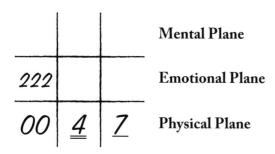

**Mental Plane**

**Emotional Plane**

**Physical Plane**

**Comments:** Introversion will be a problem here. A 3 name would open up the personality, and a 5 name would be a good alternative.

# 6

---

# THE FOURTH
# SPHERE OF INFLUENCE:
# SPHERE OF EXPRESSION

## The Whole Name

The Fourth Sphere of Influence is found by adding the numerical value of the letters of the whole name and reducing to a single digit. It indicates, on one hand, the talents we are endowed with and, on the other hand, it serves as a channel for these talents to be expressed. This sphere is also known as the Sphere of Expression and should be examined when choosing a career.

| 1 | 2 | 3 | 4 | 5 | 6 | 7 | 8 | 9 |
|---|---|---|---|---|---|---|---|---|
| A | B | C | D | E | F | G | H | I |
| J | K | L | M | N | O | P | Q | R |
| S | T | U | V | W | X | Y | Z | |

By using the above chart, we arrive at the Fourth Sphere as shown in this example:

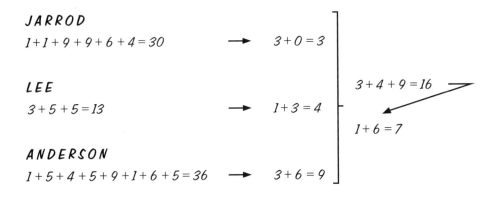

*JARROD*
$1+1+9+9+6+4=30$ $\longrightarrow$ $3+0=3$

*LEE*
$3+5+5=13$ $\longrightarrow$ $1+3=4$

$3+4+9=16$ $\longrightarrow$

$1+6=7$

*ANDERSON*
$1+5+4+5+9+1+6+5=36$ $\longrightarrow$ $3+6=9$

For this sphere, record the single digit of each name and then add the three (or more) single digits together to ascertain the final number.

In our example, a 3 given name, a 4 middle name, and a 9 surname have produced a composite number of 16, reducing to the final digit 7. This final digit is the summation of the qualities of all the individual letters of the three names. These details will be helpful when examining two or more people with the same final digit number in their whole name but who express themselves with some differences. These differences are the result of their composite numbers being formed differently, therefore causing them to possess inherent variations. For example, an individual with a final digit of 7, formed as in the name Jarrod Lee Anderson, will express his or her personality and talents differently than someone whose final digit is formed from a 4 given name, a 6 middle name, and a 6 surname, which also adds up to 16 = 7.

It may be considered fortunate if the talents an individual already possesses, which are indicated and expressed by this Fourth Sphere, are found to complement the Second Sphere of Influence (Destiny). The position will be even better if the personality type (First Sphere) is also supportive. The fulfillment of destiny will then be made much easier. A harmonious combination of these important Spheres of Influence will provide considerable support to the vocations and hobbies that should be pursued.

Hobbies and recreational activities should be considered seriously, since they provide diversification of interests. Not infrequently, an avocation takes over from the vocation and becomes the source of fame and fortune. Meanwhile, hobbies and interests can provide personal fulfillment, which may not be found in regular employment. They may also provide incentive for early retirement and the avenue for developing new interests in life.

There is little doubt that the First, Second, and Fourth Spheres of Influence need to work together for success and balance. However, if these spheres are on different planes of expression, they need not be allowed to pull the personality in opposite directions but may be used to extend the talents and widen the personality's range of expression. The three spheres clamoring for attention and motivation at the same time should be recognized and reconciled. As an example, we may consider Jarrod Lee Anderson's Fourth Sphere of Influence in relation to his birthdate, which is 12/20/1983 = 26 = 8.

A cursory glance at his 8 destiny (Second Sphere) and his 7 talents (Fourth Sphere) may indicate that they are in conflict. The highly competitive, ambitious, businesslike 8 and the reserved, uncompetitive 7 do not appear to be compatible. But a closer examination will reveal that his Two personality (First Sphere) and his talents show many shared characteristics that integrate well with assertive 8 features, especially when he finds himself in a difficult situation. His intuition will be greatly enhanced and applied successfully in his business dealings by his 7. The tact and courtesy of his 2 vibration and the penetration of his 7 can combine with the organization and method of his 8.

The central idea in this exercise is to recognize and extract the best qualities of each sphere of influence and use them as a potentially successful team. What follows is a comprehensive list of occupations relative to each number. As certain vibrations share common characteristics, though expressed differently, people influenced by sympathetic vibrations are attracted to similar types of occupations. As such, generalization is necessarily the basis in presenting a list of this nature. The occupations given under each number are the ones in which fulfillment and success will be achieved naturally and easily. After a close look at all the numbers, it can be seen that some occupations do not attract people of certain vibrations.

This occupation list can help steer us in the direction in which our natural talents lie. It can be of particular help to parents, students, and people seeking employment or change of employment.

Adults who are already employed, feel content with their jobs, and know they do them well will probably find their occupations listed under the numbers of their First, Second, or Fourth Spheres of Influence. They may also find that many jobs they have seriously considered are listed.

Those who do not enjoy their jobs and often feel as if they are square pegs in round holes should look closely at the jobs listed under the numbers of their First, Second, and Fourth Spheres of Influence. They may quite possibly see avenues of employment they have desired and hobbies they have found attractive.

We should remember that while the Fourth Sphere's main purpose is to influence our choice of occupation (paid or recreational) by providing us with certain talents, the directions Destiny points out should be our first consideration. Our second consideration should be the best combination of talents we can get together from the First and Fourth Spheres of Influence, not forgetting advantages we may have in the Sixth Sphere (outer person).

## *Occupations*

### Vibration Number 1

Airline pilots

Apiarists

Architects

Assayers

Debt collectors

Designers

Detectives

Drovers

Editors

Engineers

Entrepreneurs

Estate agents

Excavators

Executives

Explorers

Farmers

Fitness instructors

Fund-raisers (political)

Glassblowers

Inventors

Managers

Manufacturers

Mathematicians

Merchant seamen

Metallurgists

Music composers

Orchestra conductors

Overseers

Personal trainers

Pioneer farmers

Playwrights

Politicians

Printers

Producers

Promotion managers

Publishers

Ranchers

Reporters

Researchers

Scientists

Sports professionals

Tailors

Taxi drivers

Weavers

Web designers

Wine producers

## Vibration Number 2

Actors (romance)

Advertisers

Ambulance officers

Arbitrators

Bacteriologists

Ballet dancers and instructors

Beauticians

Biographers

**Vibration Number 2 (*continued*)**

Biologists

Bookbinders

Bus drivers

Calligraphers

Care workers

Childcare workers

Clerks

Collectors

Computer programmers

Correspondents

Credit officers

Curators (art galleries and museums)

Dancers and dance instructors

Data analysts

Deputies

Diplomats

Domestic servants

Dressmakers

Embroiderers

Engineers (electronics and marine)

Engravers

Entertainers

Florists

Genealogists

Glassblowers

Goldsmiths

Hairdressers

Historians

Homemakers

Hosts and hostesses

Ice skaters

IT consultants

Legal secretaries

Librarians

Mediators

Medical practitioners

Meteorologists

Musicians

Negotiators

Nurses

Opticians

Pastry cooks

Pawnbrokers

Personnel officers

Pharmacists

Photographers

Pilots (marine)

Process workers

Psychics

Receptionists

Secretaries

Shoemakers

Sign writers

Silversmiths

Social workers

Spiritual healers

Statisticians

Striptease artists

Taxi drivers

Teachers (elementary school)

Tour directors

Travel agents

Truck drivers

Waiters

Watchmakers

Writers (romance)

## Vibration Number 3

Accountants

Actors (comedians)

Advertisers

Announcers

Art critics

Art dealers

Artists

Beauticians

Beauty therapists

Cabaret artists

Cabinetmakers

Callers

Cartoonists

Choreographers

Commentators

Comperes

Cosmetics manufacturers

Decorators

Disc jockeys

Editors

Engineers (aerospace)

Entertainers (solo)

Executives

Fashion designers

Fashion models

Goldsmiths

Hairdressers

Hosts and hostesses

Illustrators

Instructors

Inventors

Jewelers

Journalists

Lawyers

Lecturers

Managers

**Vibration Number 3 (*continued*)**

| | |
|---|---|
| Mathematicians | Proofreaders |
| Military officers | Salespeople |
| Ministers (religious) | Scouts and guides |
| Motivational speakers | Sign writers |
| Musicians | Social secretaries |
| Poets | Teachers (music) |
| Politicians | Window dressers |
| Printers | Writers (short stories) |

## Vibration Number 4

| | |
|---|---|
| Accountants | Cartoonists |
| Agriculturalists | Chemists (industrial) |
| Appraisers | Clerks |
| Archaeologists | Clothiers |
| Architects | Concrete layers |
| Assayers | Credit officers |
| Auditors | Data analysts |
| Biologists | Dentists |
| Bookbinders | Draftspeople |
| Bookkeepers | Economists |
| Bricklayers | Efficiency experts |
| Business proprietors | Engineers (construction) |
| Buyers | Estimators |
| Cabinetmakers | Excavators |
| Carpenters | Farmers |

Firefighters

Fund-raisers (charity)

Geologists

Graphic designers

Hardware merchants

Horticulturalists

Joiners

Laborers

Masons

Massage therapists

Mechanics

Metallurgists

Miners

Musicians (drums and martial music)

Pawnbrokers

Physical education instructors

Plumbers

Police officers

Potters

Process workers

Protocol officers

Ranchers

Real estate agents

Safety officers

Sculptors

Security guards

Sign writers

Soldiers

Sports professionals

Statisticians

Stonemasons

Storekeepers

Surgeons

Tax consultants

Technicians

Undertakers

## Vibration Number 5

Acrobats

Actors (drama)

Administrators

Advertisers

Ambulance officers

Announcers

Bartenders

Broadcasters

Bus drivers

Cabaret artists

Chauffeurs

Circus performers (including clowns)

Coaches (sport)

Commercial travelers

## Vibration Number 5 (*continued*)

Couriers

Critics

Demonstrators

Detectives

Disc jockeys

Editors

Electrical engineers

Engineers (aeronautical)

Entrepreneurs (sports and
   entertainment)

Explorers

Fashion models

Firefighters

Freedom fighters

Fund-raisers (political and sport)

Gamblers (professional)

Gym instructors

Herder

Humorists

Illustrators

Interpreters

Investigators

Journalists (freelance)

Lawyers

Lecturers

Linguists

Lobbyists

Marketing consultants

Media representatives

Military officers

Motivational speakers

Mountaineers

Organizers

Personnel managers

Photographers

Police officers

Politicians

Promoters

Psychologists

Publishers

Racecar drivers

Salespersons

Spies

Taxi drivers

Test pilots

Tour guides

Translators

Transport executives

Travel consultants

Travelers

Unionists

Volunteer workers (specialized)

Welfare workers

Writers (controversial issues)

## Vibration Number 6

Actors (drama)

Bakers

Bartenders

Caretakers

Care workers

Caterers

Chefs

Chauffeurs

Childcare workers

Computer technicians

Connoisseurs (food, wine, fine arts)

Cooks

Counselors

Dance instructors

Dealers in cloth or clothing

Decorators

Diplomats

Domestic servants

Florists

Food and beverage managers

Girl Scout leaders

Health and safety consultants

Historians

Homemakers

Hosts and hostesses (entertainment
  and hospitality industries)

Hotel executives

Innkeepers

Lawyers

Lecturers

Lobbyists

Marriage officiants

Massage therapists

Medical practitioners

Mimes

Negotiators

Personal trainers

Personnel managers

Personnel officers

Philosophers

Poets

Restaurateurs

Scoutmasters

Servers (food and drink)

Social hosts and hostesses

Social workers

Songwriters

Storytellers

**Vibration Number 6 (*continued*)**

Teachers

Volunteers (charity)

Wine tasters

Yoga instructors

Welfare workers

## Vibration Number 7

Accountants

Antique dealers and collectors

Anthropologists

Apiarists

Archaeologists

Archivists

Artists (landscape)

Astrologers

Astronomers

Bacteriologists

Bankers

Biologists

Brewers

Brokers

Business analysts

Canoeists

Chemists

Consultants (environment)

Curators (museums)

Drovers

Engineers (biomedical)

Excavators

Farmers

Finance analysts

Finance brokers

Financiers

Fishermen

Florists

Forest rangers

Gardeners

Geographers

Geologists

Greengrocers

Historians (ancient history)

Horticulturalists

Inventors

Investigators

Investors

Laboratory workers

Lawyers

Lecturers

Lighthouse keepers

Market gardeners

Medical specialists

Meteorologists

Miners

Ministers (religious)

Music composers

Naturalists

Nurserymen

Paleontologists

Pharmacists

Poets

Poultry farmers

Private investigators

Professors

Psychiatrists

Psychoanalysts

Quality controllers

Ranchers

Real estate agents

Reiki masters

Research workers

Secret Service agents

Scientists

Statisticians

Tax consultants

University lecturers

Wine producers

Writers (science, philosophy, mystery)

Zoologists

## Vibration Number 8

Accountants

Administrators

Bankers

Brokers

Builders

Bureaucrats

Businesspeople

Buyers

Coaches (sports)

Computer programmers

Contractors

Efficiency experts

Executives

Financial counselors

Financiers

Funeral directors

Insurance (all types)

Judges

**Vibration Number 8 (*continued*)**

Lawyers (corporate)

Legislators

Managers

Manufacturers

Marketing executives

Merchants

Organizers

Politicians

Production executives

Retail managers

Shipbuilders

Sports professionals

Stockbrokers

Town planners

Treasurers

Union officials

## Vibration Number 9

Academics

Actors (tragedians)

Administrators

Announcers

Artists

Art restorers

Bacteriologists

Bus and coach drivers

Curators (museums and art galleries)

Dancers and dance instructors

Decorators

Diagnosticians

Dieticians

Diplomats

Drama teachers

Editors

Evangelists

Fashion models

Fund-raisers (charity)

Horticulturalists

Human resources consultants

Journalists

Media reporters

Medicine (all fields)

Ministers (religious)

Missionaries

Music composers

Musicians

Novelists

Orchestra conductors

Organists

Philosophers

Poets

Poultry breeders

Printers

Reiki masters

Singers

Social workers

Spiritual healers

Teachers

Travelers

Yoga instructors

## Vibration Number 11

Actors

Advertisers

Announcers

Astrologers

Astronomers

Dressmakers

Engineers (electronics, chemical, marine, and traffic)

Evangelists

Explorers (scientific and metaphysical)

Human resources consultants

Inventors

IT consultants

Lobbyists

Mediums

Meteorologists

Missionaries

Music composers

Orators

Philosophers

Pilots (marine)

Politicians

Psychics

Psychoanalysts

Psychologists

Publishers

Radio and television technicians

Reformers

Salespeople

Scientists (space)

Social workers

Songwriters

Volunteers (charity)

Writers (inspirational and scientific)

## *Vibration Number 22*

Subjects of this Master Vibration may choose any field of human endeavor and be assured of leaving their footprints behind. It is the one vibration that contains the characteristics of all others and gives its subjects the power to function with equal ease on the physical, emotional, mental, and inspirational planes.

# 7

## THE FIFTH SPHERE OF INFLUENCE: SPHERE OF THE INNER PERSON

### Vowels of the Whole Name

Among the vowels of the whole name we can find the heart of a person or, to put it another way, the subtlest aspects of the personality. This Fifth Sphere of Influence is usually referred to as the inner person. It is the sphere of inner desires, usually familiar only to the individual. (Refer to page 8 for an explanation of vowel values.)

The concealment we find here makes the Fifth Sphere the least apparent, but it is no less significant than the others. In fact, it takes precedence over the others at certain times during the life of the great majority of people. Anything that lies hidden tends to arouse curiosity and anticipation; hence, revealing the nature of this Sphere of Influence always provides surprises. It is an area of the personality closely associated with the subconscious mind, representing inner urges, promptings, desires, and longings, and is not to be taken as representing outer personality traits, accomplishments, or requirements.

The forces within this sphere, however, constantly seek outlets, and to the degree that these outlets are found and used, a well-rounded personality is achieved. If no opening is found in any one or more of the other Spheres of Influence, the personality may suffer from disillusionment and frustration until, through self-study, the situation is recognized and personal adjustments are made. Despite the fact that this is generally a concealed area, there are instances where people wear their hearts on their sleeves; these are simply the open personalities that we sometimes encounter.

There is usually a variation in the degree of influence of the Fifth Sphere's forces. These forces can be dormant, ignored or suppressed, or consciously and intelligently used, and in some instances, they can become extremely active or suddenly awakened. A sudden, inexplicable change in a seemingly established lifestyle may be the result of an abrupt awakening of these inner forces when they find a ready outlet to actively participate with the other Spheres of Influence.

The Fifth Sphere is of considerable importance when undertaking a permanent or long-term partnership of any sort, because whatever facade or feigned condition a person may temporarily assume, that person will sooner or later revert to fundamental desires.

Partners in marriage should ascertain and understand the nature of each other's inner persons for the success of the partnership. For instance, if the Fifth Sphere of one partner is influenced by the 7 vibration, which yearns for tranquility, silence, and abstract study, and the other is influenced by the outgoing 3 vibration, there will be problems sooner or later unless there is a process of sorting out, understanding, and adjusting their differences.

In order to ascertain the secrets of this intriguing sphere, the usual practice of converting the letters of the whole name to their numerical values is followed, but for this sphere, only the vowels are used. After conversion, they are added together and the compound number is then reduced to a single digit, as in the following example:

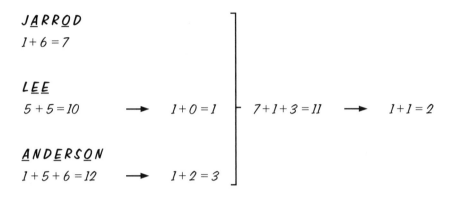

The inner person of our Mr. Anderson will feel the urge to, in his quieter moments, express the higher qualities of the Master Vibration 11 or the standard qualities of the 2. Which set will predominate will depend on other areas of influence and his life situation.

## Vibration Number 1 as Inner Person

The 1 vibration is experienced as a constant pressure on the ego to assume the general characteristics of this vibration, especially those of independence and leadership. People with this number will automatically take over and direct any situation they may find themselves in. They will find personal satisfaction only when they are giving orders and not when they are taking them. If they are not in a position of authority, they prefer to work on their own, unhampered by interference and restrictions.

The degree to which this inner compulsion is achieved will depend on the compatibility between this vibration and those in the other Spheres of Influence. If there is an opening in any one or more of the other Spheres of Influence, particularly in the First Sphere, these individuals will be capable of considerable accomplishment. Their strong inner drive will carry them through any rough patches in their lives, much to the surprise of people who are unaware of this inner strength. This trait is often revealed not only in their personal lives but also in times of any emergency, including civil disorder and warfare.

The creative forces of this vibration constantly seek means of fulfillment, and in instances where outlets do not exist for this person to be a leader, these creative forces may still provide many satisfying avenues for fulfillment. The creativity of Ones will lead them into entrepreneurial activities and careers in fashion designing. They will always be in the forefront in business and social life. In personal relationships, sooner or later they will reveal many unsuspected qualities, such as loyalty, willpower, ambition, authority, and pride. The negative personalities tend toward conceited, critical, dictatorial, and selfish behavior.

## Vibration Number 2 as Inner Person

Companionship, accompanied by love, kindliness, peace, and harmony, will be the strongest yearning of people with the 2 vibration in the Fifth Sphere. There will be no inner incitement toward competition, ambition, commercialism, and popularity through wealth and power. They will seek to cooperate, assist, support, and serve. They will often withdraw into the 2 vibration's characteristic pastime of fantasy. The positive Twos will find real enjoyment in their beautiful mental creations, while the negative ones will indulge in pessimistic and melancholy thoughts.

Their strong psychic sense constantly seeks to surface but may easily be stifled by environmental influences or by other areas of the personality that are antagonistic or indifferent to its development. The real inner strength of those with a Two as their inner person lies in their qualities of compassion, understanding, diplomacy, flexibility, and generosity, and in their absence of greed, jealousy, pride, anger, and resentment. Weaknesses such as a lack of willpower and self-discipline, indecisiveness, and excessive diffidence will be common in the more negative personalities.

### Vibration Number 3 as Inner Person

The driving forces behind this youthful vibration, such as the need for self-expression, the desire for popularity, and the zest for living, all seek outlets. These people are dreamers at heart, and their vivid imaginations impel them to seek various means through which their mental creations can be expressed. Oral expression takes first place. The desire to speak out, give orders, express opinions, and entertain will be irresistible. Threes' sense of beauty, color, creative impulses, and emotion constantly seek avenues of expression.

A close relationship with these people will soon reveal generous, joyful, optimistic, and entertaining personalities without the debilitating influences of worry, depression, and melancholy. Threes' strength and weakness both lie in their great need, not only for social intercourse but also to occupy the center position in any social gathering. The positive ones have no difficulty in achieving these desires. The negative ones usually resort to creating situations, usually unpleasant, whereby they become the center of attention. They will never want to lag behind or fall into a rut. Attempts to suppress or hold these people back will not succeed in the long run because of their constant desire to keep abreast of current happenings and to play an active part in a situation. Unless supported by other vibrations, they will not be happy if confined entirely to a domestic scene or forced into routine, detail, and monotony. If regular work does not include productive activity, their inner urges for artistic creation, social involvement, and expression of emotion will be satisfied by interests outside of their normal responsibilities.

### Vibration Number 4 as Inner Person

The enduring qualities of dependability, honesty, loyalty, and service—to family, community, and country—form the bedrock of all people with this vibration controlling the Fifth Sphere of Influence. Any attempt to enlist them to rebel against or question traditional ways of life will be firmly rebuffed. They are entirely at ease accepting and upholding the established laws and customs of the land. When committed to or enlisted in a cause, their self-discipline and self-sacrifice will soon be revealed, much to the relief of those depending on them. They are followers rather than leaders and are unlikely to question authority.

They are unable to enjoy relaxation and ease if a job needs to be done. Full inner contentment is achieved when all responsibilities have been attended to in an efficient manner. Lack of a lively imagination and resentment of change may finally disclose serious and sedate personalities, especially in personal relationships, when gaiety, frivolity, and humor have been expected. This is amply compensated, however, by the sincerity, security, and stability they provide in any relationship.

Family love and pride are fundamental to these people, who will resist with great vehemence any assaults on the security and good name of the family. Their love is deep and ironclad, though not demonstrated by a great show of emotion. Laziness and dullness will override the mentality of negative people with the 4 vibration in this sphere.

## Vibration Number 5 as Inner Person

The heart's desire of the 5 vibration is freedom of expression, which is its principal motivating force, and the need for a diversified lifestyle becomes an integral part of this freedom. Considerable disturbance in the personality will result if opportunities for freedom of expression are not available through the other Spheres of Influence or in the environment they live in. The curiosity of the 5 vibration, which is now the foundation of the personality, must also be satisfied. If not, these people will use both straightforward and devious methods to make it so.

Impatience will stir them into action. This inner restlessness must be understood and recognized by the individuals themselves and by others, and adjustment to their lifestyle made accordingly. It must be known that deep within these people lie intelligent, alert, quick-witted, and volatile personalities. Opportunities to indulge in variety should be available, especially to children, so that expansion of the inner person is not stifled.

It may not always be possible to comply with the yearning for travel, which is always present wherever the 5 vibration operates. However, this can be satisfied by a variety of literature and a vocation or avocation as a writer. The written word can be made the conduit through which the courage, restlessness, and other outward characteristics of this vibration can be expressed. Many successful freelance correspondents are subjects of this vibration.

In personal relationships, it must be recognized that the 5 is not a domestic number, and those influenced by it in any of the Spheres of Influence should not be committed entirely to such responsibilities because very little success will result.

## Vibration Number 6 as Inner Person

The 6 vibration will exercise a firm grip on the domestic life of all the people it influences. The primary urge will be for marriage and the setting up of home and family. There will be no inner contentment until their home has been established. Their concentrated energies will not only be directed toward establishing a home but also toward maintaining it, living in it, and beautifying it. They rarely feel the need for vacations elsewhere. If they do go away, their subconscious minds draw them back home and they are indeed glad to be back when their trip is over.

The high artistic appreciation of the 6 vibration is generally displayed in their homes, giving them an atmosphere of beauty, harmony, and good taste. These are extroverted people who delight in congenial company and avoid solitude. The hospitality of all true Six people is renowned. The genuine matriarchs and patriarchs who exercise a powerful yet benign influence over a large family are found within this vibration. They seek no other ambition than to lovingly control and serve their families.

All Sixes who are well established in their domestic lives are motivated by a strong urge to extend their love and personal service into the community. Strong maternal or paternal instinct to guide, counsel, and teach will be fulfilled in community activity. In personal relationships, Sixes' partners must recognize these individuals' almost total attachment to home and family. It will not be possible to influence Sixes to adopt a shifting lifestyle.

Sixes have no inner drive for competition in the commercial world. Love of good food, physical comfort, and enjoyment of artistic pleasures could be taken to extremes by the more negative types, at the expense of physical activity.

## Vibration Number 7 as Inner Person

Subjects of this vibration experience a continual pull away from social involvement and competition in the commercial world, both consciously and subconsciously. They feel a real need for silence and peace, which they find in solitude and communion with their inner selves. Strident noises and other discordant vibrations of the outer world have a detrimental effect on them. If they are constantly exposed to these disturbances, they will experience much suffering. The situation is compounded when contrasting vibrations exist in the other Spheres of Influence. For instance, individuals with a 7 inner person will suffer much inner conflict if other Spheres of Influence are ruled by extroverted, social vibrations. Their greatest problem will be to reconcile these opposing facets of their personalities. Learning to be alone and not being lonely will be one of the first adjustments.

Quite often these individuals are depressed and deeply withdrawn, and fail to realize the cause of their moods. Associates and loved ones will certainly be unable to figure out the causes, and a good deal of unnecessary misunderstanding is a result. These Sevens are not able to communicate their inner feelings to others. They find it most distasteful to expose their sentiments to others.

Sevens who are undisturbed by contrary vibrations within themselves are easily able to live alone. The absence of emotional attachments gives them the opportunity to devote themselves to spiritual evolution, which will often be their greatest wish.

## Vibration Number 8 as Inner Person

The inner urges of the 8 vibration separate them into two distinct but not dissimilar forces. On one hand, the desire to possess material wealth and power exerts pressure on the personality, and on the other, the 8 vibration's natural tendencies to lead, organize, and administer affairs and people seek to take over. The combination of these two forces inevitably produces a forceful personality if outlets for expression are present in the other Spheres of Influence.

It is not an easy inner life to cope with, as opportunities for fulfillment may not always be presented; furthermore, the destiny of an individual may point in a different direction. If one or more of the other spheres are not geared to handle these powerful forces, frustration need not necessarily be the result. Some of the strong attributes of the 8 vibration, such as enthusiasm for work, determination, dedication, and organization, can be used to achieve success in any other type of destiny, or they could be used for generally strengthening the personality type. The secret is to realize that these powers exist in the background of the personality. Although others will not recognize 8 souls based on outer appearances, they will soon do so when these people live up to all the expectations and demands of life.

## *Vibration Number 9 as Inner Person*

Stirred up by an emotional core, all inner Nines revel in high ideals and visions for the amelioration of animal and human suffering. Their impulse to think about cruelty to animals, people's inhumanity to one another, and nature's harshness to both creates within them a restlessness and a sense of urgency, followed by a need for action. These altruistic promptings often clash with their ambition and their wishes for personal enrichment through material possessions. Successful Nines overcome the drawbacks of self-centeredness, selfishness, and emotionalism, and are able to concentrate on humanitarian service. Their strongest urge is to become a universal brother or sister.

The refined vibrations animating these people give them proficiency in and love for music, art, drama, and literature, which enables them to express their fine sensitivity, high sense of beauty, and high-minded thoughts. Due to the internationalism of the 9 vibration, they instinctively regard the world as their stage and seek knowledge of and participation in the cultural pursuits of all lands. There is a strong drive to undertake frequent journeys to the cultural centers of the world and to acquire a reputation as an ambassador of learning.

The generosity of the 9 vibration constantly erupts and is displayed not in the dispensation of material largesse but in personal service as teachers, healers, humanitarians, and philanthropists. Their intense desire to give, even at the risk of their own impoverishment, leads these people into many difficult situations.

Their inner desires are not confined to cultural and humanitarian pursuits but also include spiritual evolution to a large extent. Their religious beliefs are not often traditional. Global orientation, intuition, and extrasensory perception guide them into the widest possible fields of knowledge in metaphysics and mysticism. The need to impart this knowledge is a strong urge that can consume them.

## *Vibration Number 11 as Inner Person*

The inner life of people whose vowels add up to 11 is an escalation of those represented by the number 9. This escalation applies particularly in regard to internationalism and the dissemination of spiritual knowledge. Elevens are capable of emotional detachment, unlike Nines, who are sensitive.

Elevens' inner life is spent enjoying their visions and dreams of uplifting the spiritual and moral life of humanity as a whole, with little or no concern for individuals. Their passion to reveal what they, rightly or wrongly, consider to be the true path to humanity's salvation is irresistible. This is followed by a call to evangelize. With the strength of two 1s and the support of the underlying 2, inner guidance is at its strongest with these individuals. They can safely rely upon their intuition and psychic ability. Their devotion, strength, and single-mindeness make them entirely fearless in probing the spiritual and physical realms of life and also in resisting any onslaughts on their ideals and visions.

While some inner Elevens will confine themselves to theorizing and spreading the word as they see it without practical application, others may seek to direct their considerable inner powers toward inventions that may be lasting aids to human welfare. The degree of success achieved will no doubt depend upon the other Spheres of Influence.

In negative Eleven personalities, their message is delivered in an egoistic and pedantic manner with little concern for the sensitivities and opinions of others. In intimate relationships, all Elevens, whether positive or negative, reveal themselves as serious individuals engaged in a wide spectrum of idealism with little time and concern for personal responsibilities.

### *Vibration Number 22 as Inner Person*

People activated from within by this Master Vibration of the master builder seek means for practical application of their spiritual, mental, and physical energies. They realize that thought and speech must be followed by constructive deeds. Inner Twenty-twos are so intense that they can strongly influence the lives of those around them.

The most ardent wish of all positive people with the 22 inner urge is to see a society of nations and to play a considerable part in contributing some lasting benefit to that vast organization. Their thoughts are projected to international organizations of various sorts, humanitarian societies, the construction of buildings on a large scale, roads, railways, waterways, and the development of aerial and space travel. Negative Twenty-twos, unfortunately, are insensitive to the welfare of others and direct their powerful creative thoughts toward selfish accumulation of power and wealth.

## First Vowel of the Given Name

The power of the given name's first vowel (or the first vowel of the name most often used) provides the first insight into the personality of an individual. The first vowel determines an individual's immediate impulses, responses, and reactions to all outer stimuli, and in most people, gives an instant idea of their basic personality type. Once the governing vibration of the vowel is known, the reactions of others will be understood, as well as how best to approach them.

The characteristics of the first vowel are emphasized when it is the first letter in the name and has a sound vibration of a long duration, as in Andrew or Andrea. As the second letter but still with a long duration, as in Dale or Jayne, the power of the vowel will be influenced to a degree by the vibration of the first letter, though it retains a good deal of its individual strength. The influence of the vowel is lessened when the sound is crisp, as in Roger or Jenny, and the resulting reactions are milder.

The union of two vowel sounds, as in Neal or Pauline, will complicate matters a little by the introduction of the influence of two vibrations expressed as one.

While the influence of the first vowel is helpful, it is only a cursory view of one's personality. It should not be used independently to judge people and needs to be combined with the information of as many of the Six Spheres of Influence as possible for a defined picture.

## First Vowel A (Number 1)

Reactions are mental as well as emotional, but emotions are not displayed due to the strong self-restraint of the 1 vibration that the letter *a* represents. Subject to the position of the vowel and the duration of its sound, these people will show

- Receptivity to new ideas and activities on account of the vibration's desire to create, pioneer, and explore
- A negative reaction to orders, advice, and opinions of others, since they would rather give orders, learn by experience, and voice their own opinions
- A hostile reaction to criticism or a challenge by others of their ideas, opinions, and instructions
- Strong resentment of any intrusion upon their privacy
- Intolerance of stagnant or nonprogressive views
- Accessibility only by straightforward means, and impatience and distrust of people who use a devious approach

## First Vowel E (Number 5)

Reaction to all outer stimuli is the swiftest with this vowel, owing to the 5 vibration's ever-present alertness, awareness, and inner agitation.

- As all five senses work together with this vibration, these people miss nothing. Caution should be exercised by others in speech and action when these Fives are around.
- Reactions are impulsive. Their promises and concurrences given on the spur of the moment should not be taken seriously because they could easily change their minds. They also have a strong tendency to overact and to overdramatize events.
- They are easily accessible and influenced by an emotional approach and are very receptive to novelty, variety, and intrigue.
- They display impatience to those whose thought processes and movements are slow and to those who constantly repeat themselves.
- They show strong reactions toward anyone who attempts to place any restrictions on their freedom.
- They are easily approachable by members of the opposite sex since these Fives have no inhibitions or fears.

## *First Vowel I (Number 9)*

These people use a wide perspective in their thought. Pettiness and prejudices are their pet aversions.

- Intuition, sensitivity, emotion, and refinement influence all their reactions.
- Universal standards guide all their judgments.
- They are accessible and accommodating, and easily moved by appeals for sympathy.
- Their generosity is spontaneous.
- They show instant displeasure toward aggressiveness and crudeness.

- The negative personalities produce very different reactions, such as boredom, moodiness, cynicism, and selfishness. They can be obnoxious and hurtful both intentionally and unintentionally.

## First Vowel O (Number 6)

Traditionalists and conservatives are found here. Home, family, and loved ones are their first priority. When approached along these lines, they will be congenial, hospitable, and helpful.

- They will react instantly to any danger that may face their charges.
- In all other instances, their responses are not immediate; they need to deliberate before giving their consent or opinion on any matter.
- The mental approach to these people is best, as logic governs their thoughts.
- They show irritation with emotional and erratic speech and unstable behavior.
- They will promptly raise an argument if someone's statement or opinion does not conform with facts. As a result, they often create unpleasantness although their intention is merely to help others get their facts right.
- They find it difficult to control their constant urge to teach, advise, and counsel.
- If they are motivating negatively, they are self-opinionated and dogmatic, and react fiercely to any challenge to their opinions and instructions. Their general responses are moody and melancholy.

## First Vowel U (Number 3)

A ready sense of humor forms the basis for most of their responses. These individuals are so quick at repartee that there is a need to watch what is said to them, especially by shy or sensitive people. They are always on the alert for humorous situations and will swiftly respond to an ordinary remark with a witty retort. They respond eagerly to personal love, adulation, and flattery. This will be the best approach for receiving their friendship and loyalty. The negative ones who may not receive these attentions will create situations to do so. This urgent need leads them easily into many emotional escapades and makes them prey to all types of other influences.

- Their most powerful weapon is the gift of speech, which is used generally in friendship, though they could be cutting and satirical if they choose to be.
- Their reactions are enthusiastic, optimistic, and animated. Beauty and color instantly catch their eye.
- There is no need to repeat or explain anything in detail to these people. They pick up new facts and information instantly.
- They give an instant response to pets and children.

## First Vowel Y (Number 7)

This is rarely the first vowel, but when it is, the deeper characteristics of the 7 vibration will be displayed. The names Yvonne and Yves are examples of this. (For more information on when *Y* is treated as a vowel, please refer to page 8.)

- Their aversion to frivolous and superficial people and their attraction to and admiration for deep-thinking, learned people will be obvious.
- Attempts to obtain any information from them, especially of a personal nature, usually ends in disappointment and embarrassment, for they will not reveal anything about themselves. They are enigmatic and often misunderstood.
- A display of emotion or conduct that does not conform to reason will either raise their ire or cause them to withdraw into themselves.
- Their attention and ready response is always gained if some serious or philosophical matter is broached and discussed objectively.

# 8

---

# THE SIXTH SPHERE OF INFLUENCE: SPHERE OF THE OUTER PERSON

## Consonants of the Whole Name

The existence of an inner realm within our personality must, by the law of opposites, indicate the existence of an outer realm. The single digit resulting from the sum of the consonants shows the outer, which is also referred to as the outer person. The vibrations of the physical body play a significant part in this Sphere of Influence.

This aspect of the integral personality is projected outward, both consciously and unconsciously. It is the area of first impressions and may be regarded as a facade we present to others, from which their initial judgments are made. Herein lies the importance of the Sixth Sphere of Influence. Although it is not always representative of our true selves, we should be aware of the characteristics presented by this sphere and use them consciously and honestly as a medium by which we may conduct ourselves in the most advantageous manner. The collective features of this sphere can very well be the secret of our success in the many situations we find ourselves in. It could also be used to deceive others as well as ourselves, but any success achieved by these means will be short-lived, for the true personality will emerge sooner or later.

The Sixth Sphere is the one area of our personality complex that needs constant attention and updating because it is from here that our mannerisms, speech, dress, posture, and other outward habits and idiosyncrasies are displayed. Once again, recognition, reconciliation, and balance of this Sixth Sphere with the other spheres should be a significant consideration. We need to recognize that this Outer Sphere should work in harmony with our composite personality, as determined by the other five Spheres of Influence. As such, the Sixth Sphere should reflect this whole identity rather than simply aligning itself with frequently changing fashions and conventions, which may not always suit our personalities.

The inner and outer spheres of influence should always be considered in conjunction with each other. The outer person can be quite deceiving, as it often serves consciously and unconsciously to obscure the inner person.

Individuals who possess an attractive outer person (and know it) may, by all means, take advantage of its gifts. However, if these gifts are not backed up by vibrations in the other Spheres of Influence, they will eventually overplay their part or fail to live up to expectations. On the other hand, people realizing that their outer person may be unattractive and dull may fail to sell themselves, though they may have many talents. We also encounter people whose outer and inner spheres of influence are of the same numbers. These are straightforward personalities who are in fact exactly what they appear to be.

The following words from Robert Burns's "Lines to a Louse" come to mind when discussing this Outer Sphere:

> O wad some Power the giftie gie us
> To see oursels as ithers see us!
> It wad frae monie a blunder free us
> An', foolish notion ...

In order to ascertain the outer person of Jarrod Lee Anderson, we convert the consonants of his whole name as follows:

*JARROD*
$1 + 9 + 9 + 4 = 23$  $\longrightarrow$  $2 + 3 = 5$

*LEE*
$3$

$5 + 3 + 6 = 14$  $\longrightarrow$  $1 + 4 = 5$

*ANDERSON*
$5 + 4 + 9 + 1 + 5 = 24$  $\longrightarrow$  $2 + 4 = 6$

With the number 5 controlling his outer person, Jarrod projects an image of an alert, active, inquisitive, and friendly individual. Unless he is supported by other areas of influence, these features will not be a true image of his personality. The fact is, other areas of influence do not contribute the same attributes in any degree of strength. The 2 vibration forming his basic personality and the 2 of his inner personality are gentle and sensitive forces, and are not as outgoing and exuberant as the 5. These will prevent him from maintaining the pace and demands of a 5 condition. In addition, his Fourth Sphere of Influence is governed by a 7, which is also a genteel vibratory force, similar to the 2 in many ways. People influenced by the 7 in any sphere of influence are not interested in projecting themselves in society in order to gain popularity.

## Vibration Number 1 as Outer Person

Those whose outer person is governed by this vibration will project typical 1 vibration qualities of individuality, authority, willpower, resourcefulness, courage, and new ideas.

Their speech and general manner will be direct and matter-of-fact, and their individuality will also be reflected in their attire, which will always be neat, stylish, personal, and exclusive.

They will quickly attract the regard and acceptance of others who share their 1 characteristic. However, a corresponding backup by similar vibrations in the other Spheres of Influence will be needed in order to maintain the personality type projected. If not, there will be a letdown in a crisis, leading to failure and disappointment.

## Vibration Number 2 as Outer Person

The effects produced on others will be a fine mixture of refinement, gentleness, tact, patience, and harmony. People will feel comfortable in the presence of these nonaggressive personalities and feel reassured by their presence, as they would of associates or helpers.

The impression of kindliness and understanding these personalities exude make them popular in social life. Strongly confident, extroverted characters are instantly attracted to these types. They are soft-spoken, graceful, and rhythmic in their movements, and look their best in garments made of soft, flowing materials.

## Vibration Number 3 as Outer Person

These individuals are seen as friendly, good-humored, vivacious, and entertaining; they are depended upon to lead the conversation in any gathering. Not surprisingly, they find themselves the center of attention, lifting the atmosphere to a level that gives pleasure to all those present. They project high intelligence, alertness, youthfulness, and camaraderie. This appearance has many demands placed on it, especially in the social scene.

Always fashionably dressed, many Threes are known for their outrageous styles, accessories, and colors. Their artistic flair and youthful deportment make them look good in almost any style and color.

## Vibration Number 4 as Outer Person

A composite image of respectability, conservatism, and patriotism is projected by people with this outer aspect. Also, on account of their dependability, practicality, and common sense, there is a comfortable and secure atmosphere around them that influences many people to attach themselves to these Four personalities.

Their honest and kindly manner may be somewhat colored by sternness, self-discipline, and forthright speech. Healthy physical energy dedicated to work and service to others is their most prominent feature. Others will place great trust and reliance in them. The clothing they choose will be for durability and quality rather than for color or fashion.

## Vibration Number 5 as Outer Person

The reputation of these people as the greatest talkers will be well known. Enthusiasm, emotion, wit, and repartee characterize their speech, making them influential and interesting conversationalists. Others rely on them to keep the conversation alive in any gathering. The more negative ones can carry this gift of speech too far and plunge headlong into discussing matters they know very little about.

They project strong personal magnetism and sensuality and other typical traits of the 5 vibration such as impulsiveness, daring, and nervous energy. A fast turnover in relationships can be expected. While they are easily bored and seek change, many people may find it wearisome to put up with their highly tensed vibrations for very long.

As leaders of fashion they are well dressed and often display the daring of the 5 vibration in their choice of clothes and color.

## Vibration Number 6 as Outer Person

The paternal or maternal look distinguishes the Six outer person from others. Sympathy and understanding are expressed in their speech and manner. People of all ages do not hesitate to seek their company, for they are seen as basically good people who are approachable and helpful. And since all Sixes love to be of service to others, they will never disappoint or rebuff anyone. Their patience, tact, and diplomacy give them the ability to handle all types of people.

In dress, they are more concerned with comfort than following the latest fashions. Garments of good quality and simple styles will be their choice, rather than anything intricate and fussy.

## Vibration Number 7 as Outer Person

People with Seven outer personalities stand out in a crowd with their aloofness and poise. An air of mystery and distance surrounds them. As their oral communication is strictly controlled, very little is known about their thoughts. They give an impression of inapproachability and exclusiveness and, as a result, are often misunderstood by those who do not know them well. Unfair interpretations often are placed on their manner and speech, especially their indifference to casual conversation.

All Seven outer personalities unconsciously project an image, often quite justifiably, of being intelligent and knowledgeable people. They will not be seen in flashy clothes and gaudy colors. Sober colors and quality materials will be their choice.

## *Vibration Number 8 as Outer Person*

Eight outer persons will display an image of prosperity, success, authority, and power, plus many of the popular characteristics of the 8 vibration. As a result, these personalities frequently find themselves in positions of authority and responsibility. However, they need to be backed up by supportive inner vibrations and other strong personality traits. If not, the strong facade they project will be no more than a false front leading to an inevitable letdown. If there is good support, openings for advancement and success will always be offered to them.

They are conservative in their choice of clothing, and regardless of their circumstances, they dress in a manner that conveys an aura of prosperity.

## *Vibration Number 9 as Outer Person*

These individuals project personal magnetism without the slightest degree of aggression or egotism. They are seen as kindly and world-wise people who are understanding, approachable, and welcome in any gathering for their wide knowledge and conversational skills.

Their innate wisdom and ability to fraternize easily attracts all types of people who, no matter what their status, feel comfortable and eager in the presence of Nines, rather than inferior and uninformed.

All Nines are seen as emotional and romantic people, and could have many admirers among the opposite sex. Their internationalism is also seen in their dress. They do not hesitate to wear anything that is comfortable, dramatic, colorful, and artistically put together.

## *Vibration Number 11 as Outer Person*

Depending on the presence or absence of stability in the other Spheres of Influence, these Elevens will appear either as inspirational, mystical, and high-minded or as dreamers, fanatics, soapbox preachers, and phonies. Whether positive or negative in outlook, all Elevens will make use of every opportunity to give vocal expression to their insights and opinions, which are always ahead of the times and even revolutionary. They do not hesitate to express strong opinions on equality of the sexes and equal opportunity. Their tendency toward exaggeration and elaboration is well known to their listeners. As originators rather than followers, particularly in the fine arts, their individuality is seen in their clothing. Most Elevens would prefer to make or design their own clothes so that their artistic flair may be given expression.

## *Vibration Number 22 as Outer Person*

Positive personalities with a 22 vibration controlling their outer image will be seen as commanding personalities with an aura of power and control over all situations. They also display physical and mental energy, practicality, efficiency, and expertise in any field. They are familiar figures in the international scene, dressed in the highest-quality clothing in conservative styles, and always appearing successful and wealthy.

This is a difficult facade for the average personality to maintain. The vibrations of the Four outer person are seen in those who are unable to keep up with the high image of this Master Vibration.

\* \* \*

This chapter completes the information on the Six Spheres of Influence. By analyzing the details presented by each sphere, one can create a complex, composite image of the person being studied. It is always important to develop an understanding of the inter-relations of the numbers and the way particular numbers in combination have particular ways of influencing each other. We have outlined many factors that affect the relationships of the numbers. These include the presence or absence of the 1 vibration, the repetition of numbers, conflict between particular Spheres of Influence, conflict between planes of expression, the absence of numbers in particular areas of the Birth Grid, and similarities between numbers.

The following chapters are designed to help develop greater insight into the relationships of the numbers, which in turn will strengthen our ability to make more accurate numerological assessments of the people we meet.

# 9

---

# THE SIGNIFICANCE OF THE
# LETTERS OF THE WHOLE NAME

The letters of the whole name fulfill another important function; they contribute complementary sets of vibrations that should be considered in relation to those of the birthdate. Although their influence is not as powerful as the First, Second, and Third Spheres of Influence, they contribute significantly to the personality as a whole. The letters, with their corresponding number values, can provide areas of power that are not found in the birthdate, strengthen vibrations existing in the birthdate, or overload an individual with a particular vibration.

The numerological grid is again used to set up a picture using the letters/numbers of the whole name. We record the number of times each letter/number appears and then consider the pattern that has unfolded, as in the following example:

# JARROD LEE ANDERSON

## *Date of birth: 12/20/1983 = 26 = 8*

**BIRTH GRID**

| | |
|---|---|
| *3* | *9* |
| *22* | *88* |
| *110* | |

Mental Plane

Emotional Plane

Physical Plane

*JARROD LEE ANDERSON*
*119964 355 15459165*

Number of times vibrations appear in the whole name:

| Vibration | Quantity of Letters |
|:---:|:---:|
| 1 | 4 |
| 2 | 0 |
| 3 | 1 |
| 4 | 2 |
| 5 | 5 |
| 6 | 2 |
| 7 | 0 |
| 8 | 0 |
| 9 | 3 |

**FIXED GRID**                    **NAME GRID**

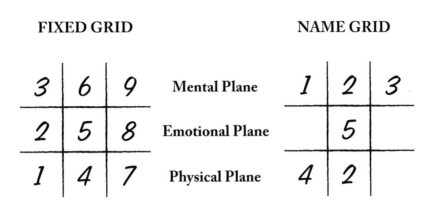

| | | | |
|---|---|---|---|
| 3 | 6 | 9 | Mental Plane |
| 2 | 5 | 8 | Emotional Plane |
| 1 | 4 | 7 | Physical Plane |

We may now consider the grid of the whole name with the grid of the birthdate and see what advantages and disadvantages are contained within the letters of the whole name. We also take into consideration the horizontal and vertical areas.

The physical plane has received the added strength of 6 vibrations (four 1s and two 4s). This is most advantageous, as they provide a nice balance between the emotional and the physical planes.

The emotional plane has been given a boost by the addition of the 5 vibration five times. This vibration is not present in the birthdate; therefore, it is an important addition, as the extroverted 5 will help overcome much of the shyness and diffidence of the strong 2.

The mental plane has also been given a boost by the addition of six vibrations: one 3, two 6s, and three 9s. Overall, the horizontal plane has provided a good balance to the personality.

The first vertical area (1, 2, 3) that was strong in the birthdate has been further strengthened with four 1s and one 3, but not to the degree that it will introduce negative features. Self-assurance and self-centeredness have been increased. The absence of the 2 is good because a wider emotional outlet is not needed.

The nine letters that fall into the middle vertical area (4, 5, 6) make up the best feature of Jarrod's Name Grid, with two 4s, five 5s, and two 6s. It turns much of the self-centeredness of the first vertical line to an awareness of the needs of others and a community consciousness.

The vibrations 7, 8, and 9 in the third vertical area provide a wide outlook on life, beyond self, beyond community and country, expanding into the international scene. The 7 and 8 are not present in Jarrod's whole Name Grid, and the three 9s that are present are not enough to compensate for the absence of the 7 and 8. This is by no means a negative condition, but Jarrod's outlook on life may be restricted to self, family, community, and country.

In the following pages, each number from 1 to 9 is taken in turn and their influence in the whole Name Grid in connection to the Birth Grid is described. The effect the name has in balancing and harmonizing the birthdate or compounding its problems is detailed. These interpretations emphasize the importance of making a careful choice when selecting a name for a baby and the problems that may be alleviated if adults choose to change their name to help balance their birthdate.

It is always better to choose a name whose number is not repeated in the birth day, birth month, or destiny, as this will cause overloading. A number not present in these spheres will create other openings for the child and create better balance. However, some numbers possess similar characteristics, so the loss or absence of the qualities of a particular vibration need not be total. For instance, the absence of the 3 vibration indicates difficulties with oral expression, but this will be compensated for if the 5 vibration is found in strength. Also, it should be noted that, while the absence of a number in the birth chart can be rectified by an abundance of this number in the whole Name Grid, the abundance of a number in both grids will result in negative traits of that particular number being expressed.

## *Vibration Number 1 (A, J, S)*

People whose birthdates do not have the 1 vibration present in any degree of strength will find it most advantageous if their names have a total of three or four letters that convert to this number. In the following example, neither the birthdate nor the surname provide the desirable 1 vibration, except the weak number 1 found in the century of the full date. But a wise choice of the given name and middle name has equipped the personality with a total of four letters of the 1 vibration:

# SUSAN JOYCE HUNTER

## *Date of birth: 3/24/1984 = 31 = 4*

SUSAN  JOYCE  HUNTER
1 1 1       1

This individual will not miss out on the driving force of the primeval vibration and its many other fundamental characteristics, such as independent thought, ambition, leadership, and above all, confidence.

Generally, the absence of this number in both the birthdate and letters of the whole name will cause problems, but before a final opinion is formed, an additional search should be made for its presence or absence in the other Spheres of Influence. For instance, this vibration as the outer person in the Sixth Sphere of Influence will not carry the individual very far, but as the inner person, their Fifth Sphere, it means that strong personality traits are present deep within and may eventually break through.

The total absence of the 1 vibration is an indication of an inferiority complex and a dormant ego. Because they do not trust themselves, these people will lack initiative, ambition, and independence, and automatically become followers who will gladly let others make their decisions for them. The younger ones will be dominated and influenced at home and school—a situation that will not boost their self-esteem. With maturity, though, they may eventually acquire some measure of self-confidence and self-sufficiency.

## *Vibration Number 2 (B, K, T)*

The best attributes of the 2 vibration will be present in a whole name containing any of these three letters—*B*, *K*, and *T*. The ability to see an opposite point of view and to cooperate will be the principal advantages. Other qualities, such as tact, diplomacy, friendliness, and sensitivity, will also be contributed and will be most beneficial in the case of birthdates with many active numbers showing aggression.

If the 2 vibration is strong in the First Sphere of Influence and is also found in abundance in the whole name—that is, four or more letters—sensitivity and emotionalism will tend to be emphasized. It could lead to overemphasized sensitivity in men and extreme shyness and abnormal fears in women. However, both sexes will have a strong feeling for beauty and delicacy in all things and will express many talents in the fine arts.

The absence of understanding and cooperation, lack of consideration, and tactlessness are failings in people who do not have this vibration in their birthdates or names. Lessons they need to learn are attention to detail and punctuality. The situation is alleviated to some extent in a positive Six personality (First Sphere of Influence).

## *Vibration Number 3 (C, L, U)*

Self-expression through the gift of speech and a sense of humor are noteworthy characteristics of people with these letters in proportion. Talent will also be displayed in the creative arts. Imagination, inspiration, creativity, gaiety, and optimism will be basic qualities.

People with an abundance of these letters—four or more—may take the good qualities of the 3 vibration to extremes and lose a sense of balance and responsibility. Their energies may be dissipated and emotional disturbances revealed in extreme talkativeness. Self-centeredness and waywardness may be reflected in all their thoughts and actions.

The lack of the 3 vibration in the names, with no support in the birthdate, results in the absence of many desirable 3 attributes. A strong 5 vibration will help overcome difficulties experienced in oral expression and social intercourse. If the 1 vibration is not strong in the overall structure, these people will choose to undersell themselves rather than make any attempt at self-promotion.

## *Vibration Number 4 (D, M, V)*

People with mentally and emotionally oriented vibrations in their birthdates benefit considerably from the letters *d*, *m*, and *v* in their names. Three to four letters of the 4 vibration give them balance, a sense of values, willingness to perform physical tasks, and the ability to handle money wisely and with practicality.

An abundance of these letters, especially if the number 4 is strong in the birthdate, will produce stubbornness, narrow-mindedness, and lack of imagination.

If the names do not provide this vibration and there is no support in the birthdate, the direct result will be a dislike and fear of physical work or any activity that requires orderly manual effort. These individuals will develop a slipshod attitude and avoid systems, timetables, and routines. They will resort to shortcuts in order to overcome or minimize attention to basic duties. The affairs of these people are usually in a state of confusion, and as a result, they may resort to escapism. The presence of the 1 vibration or the 7 will help overcome some of these problems.

## Vibration Number 5 (E, N, W)

As the only vibration that communicates with every facet of the personality, a generous proportion of letters is needed before it is strong enough to reach out and influence the personality as a whole. Four to six letters will see the effects of its general features, the best being the capacity to handle an active life involving change, travel, and experience.

People whose names do not contain these letters or who only have one or two of these letters have real problems with motivation and involvement in activity of any form. Curiosity, which is natural to human nature, is not found in these people. They also suffer from lack of tolerance and are stolid and inadaptable. They become introverted and constantly seek seclusion, content to live totally dull and negative lives. Their fear of the opposite sex is considerable. In short, they find it extremely difficult to adapt to ordinary living. Life usually forces them out of their lethargy and fears to some extent, though they will continue to suffer much internal turmoil.

Misuse of personal freedom, possibly resulting in hurting others, will be a problem with those with an overabundance of 5s in their birthdate as well as their names. The desire for a variety of sensual experiences is very strong in these people.

## *Vibration Number 6 (F, O, X)*

A total of three of these letters will see the loving nature of the 6 vibration displayed at its best and will ensure its natural capacity for domestic harmony, responsible parenthood, teaching, and community service.

An excess of these letters, unfortunately, brings a rigid, unyielding attitude. Self-righteousness becomes a real problem, along with being overly concerned with domestic issues.

People whose names are without these letters will show irresponsibility in the domestic scene. The fear of being tied down and abnormal concern for self will provide genuine problems for these people. There will be little or no understanding, tolerance, or sympathy in their roles as partners, parents, or guardians. They will have to make many personal adjustments in order to succeed as marriage partners and community-conscious citizens. They will need to learn to give, especially of them-selves, before they can expect to receive. This situation will be relieved somewhat if the personalities are controlled by positive 2 or 4 vibrations.

## *Vibration Number 7 (G, P, Y)*

These letters do not occur frequently. One or two may be regarded as proportionate. The presence of these letters stirs the intuitive faculty, which in turn influences the thoughts and actions of the individual. There is an instinctive acceptance of Divinity and a spiritual basis for all existence. The 7 vibration's love of analysis, research, and clear-cut facts will also be present. An excess of these letters is rare. If found, they would force the individual to withdraw from society and resort to some form of escapism.

Unless support is found in the birthdate, the absence of faith and indifference to spiritual values leading to a fear of the nonmaterial are familiar characteristics of those who have none of these letters in their name.

A mental laziness may be present insofar as all abstract matters are concerned. They may also prove to be disinterested in their spirituality or personal faith. These people are often jolted out of their lethargy by a sudden personal calamity, which may force them to turn inward for questioning and guidance. This inward search may eventually yield faith in more enduring values and help them overcome their fear, skepticism, and doubt. These negative tendencies can be overcome if support is found with a birthdate that includes a 6, 7, 9, 11, or 22.

## Vibration Number 8 (H, Q, Z)

These are also letters that do not occur frequently. However, two to three are needed for an individual to have the 8 vibration's basic attributes. A good sense of values in the material world, backed up by good judgment, will be the main contributions.

The ambitions of people with an abundance of these letters will exceed their capabilities and opportunities. They will experience constant anxiety in their attempts to keep abreast of their ambition's demands.

As judgment is one of the strongest attributes of the 8 vibration, the absence of this vibration shows poor judgment in most matters, particularly in finance. People in this situation have no control or competence in the disposition of their income and other assets. Financial problems will always be present until circumstances force them to learn proper management of their affairs and to live within their means. The 4 or the 7 vibration in control of the personality will overcome poor judgment in these matters.

## *Vibration Number 9 (I, R)*

A total of two or three of these letters is adequate to provide the 9 vibration's most important attributes of humanitarianism and internationalism.

An abundance of either or both of these letters, which is not common, will cause fear and excessive concern for the problems of the world. Such people have a dismal outlook that spreads bad vibrations around, affecting their own health and the well-being of those associated with them.

Self-centeredness is the problem with people who have missed out on these letters. They have little or no understanding of the human aspects of life and prefer to remain detached from the troubles of others. Suffering will not move them. This situation is overcome to some extent by the presence of a good proportion of the 6 vibration in the names. Personal relationships will also be difficult, owing to hardened emotional attitudes. Unless these individuals begin to soften from within and accept involvement with people, sharing their joys and sorrows, a lonely life will be their lot.

# 10

---

# THE COMPATIBILITY OF NUMBERS

This final chapter contains brief comments on the compatibility of numbers in relation to business and personal associations. It is meant to be an instant guide only, and if an elaboration of these comments is required, reference should be made to the chapters on the First, Second, and Fifth Spheres of Influence.

When a comparison is made between two people to ascertain the degree of compatibility, particular care should be taken to confine the examination only to corresponding spheres. The First Sphere of one should be compared with the First Sphere of the other, or the Fifth Sphere of one with the Fifth Sphere of the other, and so on. The mixing of spheres will only cause confusion.

A much deeper study into the number pattern will be required to discover whether some measure of compatibility exists or can be developed, if similar numbers are found in different spheres. For instance, compatibility cannot be taken for granted if John is a type Six (First Sphere) and Helen is a Six in her inner person (Fifth Sphere). John's 6 characteristics will actively control his personality, while in Helen they will be in a passive state, or in a condition of yearning only, and may remain so if her personality type is a Five.

The personality type (First Sphere) with the aid of the outer person (Sixth Sphere) is for the most part responsible for initial attraction, which more often than not may develop into a long-term association. However, to be certain of this development, compatibility of the vibrations of the inner person (Fifth Sphere) should be checked. These two spheres are also tied up with the Sphere of Destiny (Second Sphere). All three spheres are therefore equally important and need to be considered together to ascertain the degree of compatibility and the amount and type of adjustments that invariably have to be made.

# One

## One and One

This is an unlikely and undesirable combination in a personal relationship. In the event of this occurring, the relationship will not go beyond its incipient stage. Two strong-willed and independent people will not be prepared to surrender any part of their individuality to each other. A personality clash is certain. However, a business partnership could be made very successful if each party has independent functions and they work together only when competing with others.

## One and Two

There is a magnetic attraction between people influenced by these respective active and receptive vibrations. One will complement the other by providing what the other does not possess and therefore needs. A strong bond will develop between these two once each other's role is understood. It is an excellent combination in both personal and business partnerships.

## One and Three

In personal relationships, problems are inevitable between these ego-centered individuals. Competition between the two will be constant. Both parties will give orders. The One will not tolerate the easy lifestyle of the Three, and the Three, in turn, will not stand by and accept the dominance of the One. However, this combination could be a powerful force in business, provided they have departments of their own, with the Three taking the reins in the foreground and the One holding power in the background.

## One and Four

This is a very workable relationship in personal life as well as in business. The One will respect the dependability, practicality, and honesty of the Four, while the Four will happily follow the creativity and decisiveness of the One. A strong bond will be forged between them once the One has learned to tolerate the deliberation of the Four and the Four has become accustomed to the rapid thought processes of the One.

## One and Five

A powerful and successful combination can be formed here, both in business and personal life. The extroverted and alert Five complements the inventive One. The One will produce while the Five organizes, advertises, and sells. Fear of any sort will not influence their activities. Their lives could develop into a great adventure. The Five should respect the One's individuality and take care not to organize this partner's life. The One should not attempt to restrict the freedom of movement that is inherent in the Five.

## One and Six

A worthwhile relationship can be worked out with this combination. Rough edges found in the personalities of many Ones can be removed by the genial and culture-loving Sixes. The Six will appreciate the support the One is certain to give in the domestic scene. The Six should be careful not to confine the One to an excess of domesticity. Many arguments will arise in this relationship due to the logic of the Six and the single-mindedness of the One. A successful business partnership can be achieved. Both parties will use their heads instead of their hearts in all their dealings.

## One and Seven

There is a natural attraction here, and one of the strongest possible associations can be formed once each party understands each other's individuality and need for privacy. One party should not be too demanding of the other. The One in particular should refrain from the natural urge to give orders. Success of their association will be built upon mutual respect of each other's mental ability and efficiency.

## One and Eight

This could be a disastrous personal combination unless fundamental adjustments are made. Both parties will seek to establish power and authority over the other. On the other hand, this could be formed into the most powerful of all business associations, with each having an area of responsibility for the exercise of their expertise.

## One and Nine

After some mutual adjustments, a wide-ranging and fruitful association can be achieved by these two personalities whose numbers are placed at the opposite ends of the number spectrum. The ideas of the ego-centered One will clash with the universal Nines. Yet the wisdom and understanding of the Nine can temper and absorb the One's head-on drive for personal gain.

## One and Eleven

This is an improbable combination. The physically and materially oriented One will not put up with the idealism and impracticality of the Eleven. The Eleven's attempts to reform the One's attitudes will be treated with scorn. The Eleven will find it difficult to cope with the self-centeredness and acquisitive traits of the One.

## One and Twenty-Two

This is a powerful combination. The One will find that they have met more than their match. They will accept the genius of the positive Twenty-two, and the Twenty-two in turn will appreciate and use the initiative and energy of the One. This will turn out to be a combination of the Inventor and Builder.

# Two

## Two and One

*See One and Two on page 184.*

## Two and Two

These are birds of a feather. Mutual understanding, giving and receiving, peace and harmony, and much happiness will combine to form a great personal relationship. On the negative side, both parties will lack decisiveness and self-assertiveness. For these reasons, a business association should be avoided, unless a third party who is a One, Three, or Five is included.

## Two and Three

A rewarding association can be formed once both parties understand their mutual need for personal attention—the Three to be deferred to and the Two to be cared for. The Two's shyness, sensitivity, and reticence must be understood and accepted by the Three. The active, extroverted Three can work successfully with the behind-the-scenes activity of the Two—the Three being the go-getter and the Two the quiet achiever. The Three's flirtatious nature will cause some concern to the Two in a permanent relationship. However, the Two is not entirely immovable in emotional matters if a third party uses strong persuasion.

## Two and Four

A comfortable and stable association is assured, for these two have many characteristics in common. In addition, the imagination and fluidity of the Two will help open up the stay-put attitudes of the Four. The Four, in turn, will bring stability into the emotional life of the Two. Competition will not exist between them. One will always try to help the other. Success can be achieved both in personal and business relationships.

## Two and Five

Problems are inevitable between these two emotionally charged personalities—one sensitive and easily hurt, the other volatile and callous of the other's feelings. The speed of the Five will bewilder the placid Two. The Five will not give the constant personal attention the Two needs. In turn, the Two's personal demands and attempts to restrict freedom of movement will irritate the Five. If any measure of success is attained in this association it will be the result of the Two's adjustments.

## Two and Six

Love of peace and harmony will act as a magnet to bring these two together. There will be no competition here, nor will one try to overrule the other. Love of home, plus mutual interests in healing and other cultural pursuits, will be their strongest bond. The logic of the Six will steady the sentimentality of the Two, while the Two will give cooperation and understanding to the Six. Personal happiness is assured. Success in business is also certain if they confine themselves to the many areas where they share expertise.

## Two and Seven

This is a promising combination. A few minor adjustments will be needed. The Two will have to become accustomed to the Seven's need for periods of solitude and the Seven's distaste for constant talk. The Seven should be tolerant of the Two's displays of emotion. The psychic talents of the Two will be appreciated by the mystic Seven. A common interest in the inner side of life will hold them together with greater strength than any association based on physically and materially oriented bonds. One will give strength to the other, since no competition will exist. Decision making, however, will be left to the Seven.

## Two and Eight

The Two must be prepared to be overshadowed by the Eight's protective and patriarchal or matriarchal attitudes. If this is done, a successful relationship in personal life and business can be established—the Eight as the outgoing, active provider and the Two as the busy supporter behind the scenes. The Eight will soon recognize and appreciate their dependence on the quiet strength of the Two.

## Two and Nine

The Two may suffer in a personal relationship with the Nine. Their demands for personal attention and other domestic obligations will not be met as often as they desire by the high-minded, internationally oriented Nines. The Nine will find the Two rather tiring and confining. For harmony to be maintained in personal relationships, the Two will need to elevate their ideas and overcome self-interest.

A business association, however, can be successful without many personal adjustments. The Nine will come to depend on the Two's love of routine, method, and detail.

## Two and Eleven

As with a Nine, the Two will be overshadowed by the enthusiasm and zeal of the missionary Eleven. The psychic side of the Two will appreciate the message of the Eleven, but their speed may be too much for the gentle and home-loving Two.

## Two and Twenty-Two

This is a good combination, where the straightforward Two will support the many-sided Twenty-two in a number of practical ways, especially in looking after routine but essential duties. The Twenty-two will appreciate the value of the Two and use tact and encouragement to extract the best out of the Two. The Two will, in turn, feel comforted and fulfilled in the service of the powerful Twenty-two.

# Three

## Three and One

*See One and Three on page 185.*

## Three and Two

*See Two and Three on page 188.*

## Three and Three

A life of excitement, social adventure, and fulfillment of artistic talents is certain to follow the coalition of these extroverted and mentally active types. This will, however, portray only one side of the coin, as it were. On the other side, problems will arise involving the day-to-day functions of life. One will leave the responsibility to the other. Both parties will spend their money freely. Lack of planning and thought for the future will bring about circumstances that will place considerable pressure on this association. As both parties have free and independent natures, neither will be prepared to assume a secondary role. This is fundamentally a difficult association.

## Three and Four

Immediate conflict can be expected from these basically different personalities. On the other hand, a partnership of exceptional balance and productivity can be developed if these basic differences are respected and used in a process of give and take. The Three must appreciate the practicality of the Four while understanding their lack of imagination. The Four should take advantage of the Three's creative ideas. If the Three values the gifts of the Four, they will not find them tiresome. The Four, in turn, should lift themselves up to appreciate the sense of humor and joy of living offered by the Three.

A strong combination in business as well as in personal life can be established with strength in the foreground and background of activity if these basic adjustments are made.

## Three and Five

As this is a volatile combination, constant verbal battles are inevitable. In spite of frequent differences of opinion, Three and Five will be drawn to each other by mutual interests in travel and the pursuit of pleasure, and particularly the mental challenges one will constantly hold out to the other. It is a productive combination in all forms of public entertainment. A third party will be needed to look after the practical aspects of life, as Three and Five will show no interest or capacity to look after routine and mundane responsibilities. They are both big spenders, and money will go out as fast as it comes in. Both parties are fond of gambling. This creates a generally undesirable partnership from the point of view of domestic stability.

## Three and Six

In the domestic scene, these two mentally oriented parties will find understanding sooner or later, but clashes may be expected initially. The outgoing ways of the society-loving Three may be stifled by the home-loving Six. However, as both types are fond of entertainment—one outside the home and the other within the home—no great difficulties will be experienced in adjusting themselves to each other's tastes. Furthermore, a healthy and eager exchange of conversation and artistic interests will bring about a most enjoyable relationship. Business associations, particularly in the entertainment and hospitality industries, can be very successful. The charm and initiative of the Three will be guided by the logic and balance of the Six.

## Three and Seven

In personal relationships, a tremendous effort will be needed to form some degree of compatibility between these two different personality types. The talkative and extroverted Three will not understand the contemplative and aloof Seven. The Seven, in turn, will not tolerate the constant chatter of the Three or bother with their social needs and sentimental demands. Both parties will be scornful of each other's attitudes.

A successful business association, however, can be formed. The intuition and efficiency of the Seven, particularly in financial affairs, and the charm and oral gifts of the Three can combine well to produce a profitable partnership. There will be a mutual recognition of each other's high intelligence though their thoughts are directed into different channels.

## Three and Eight

This is a combination that augurs trouble in personal relationships but could produce a formidable partnership in business. In private life, the Three will find the Eight too authoritative, and the Eight's dedication to work with little time left for play will leave the Three high and dry. The Eight, for their part, will find their Three partner hard to keep up with. The social involvements of the Three will be too much for the hard-working Eight. There will also be constant bickering over money matters. However, in business, each could occupy an area where maximum use can be made of each other's talents. The corporate power of the Eight and the agile mind of the Three can combine to produce an extraordinary association.

## Three and Nine

The quality of practicality will be conspicuous by its absence among these mentally oriented personalities. Excess of idealism and generosity make this a poor business combination. However, a rich personal relationship can emerge from this association after an initial period of adaptation. As the ego of the Three is very strong, and as the Nine has emerged out of self-centeredness into wider perspectives, some adjustments will be needed, particularly on the part of the Three. The Three will need to rise to the level of the Nine's internationalism. The Nine's compassion and understanding will encourage the Three's efforts. The Three's initial attempts to dominate the Nine will ultimately prove futile. Eventually, a fine association can be formed through their mutual interests in travel, the fine arts, and other cultural activities.

## Three and Eleven

As for the Three and the Nine, impracticality will be a problem for these two. However, the Three and Eleven will enjoy each other's company, since both are compulsive talkers and will not run out of subjects to talk about. There will be some opposition between the impersonal attitudes of the Eleven and the personal or ego-centered nature of the Three. The creative and inventive abilities of both parties will be put to maximum advantage. The domestic side of life, as well as other mundane issues, will be neglected.

## Three and Twenty-Two

This is an unlikely combination. If it does occur, the Three will be overshadowed by the Twenty-two. The Twenty-two, in turn, will find the Three immature. The Three should expect to take a subordinate position here. If this position is accepted, the Three will fulfill their own desires, since the Twenty-twos have the capacity to provide them with all the opportunity they need to do so.

## Four

## Four and One

*See One and Four on page 185.*

## Four and Two

*See Two and Four on page 188.*

## Four and Three

*See Three and Four on page 192.*

## Four and Four

Except for any differences in their background conditioning, there will be very little to be sorted out between these naturally compatible people. A partnership of tremendous strength can be formed, since both parties will be working toward the same aims. There will be coalition instead of competition. Achievement in the business world or in private life is assured. They will enjoy much personal happiness and gain the respect of the community they live in. The risk of gradually slipping into a rut in their style of living should be watched for and avoided. If this is allowed to happen, it will be an unfortunate waste of talents.

## Four and Five

These two make a combination fraught with many difficulties. Fundamental adjustments will be needed before any harmony is enjoyed, especially in personal relationships. The Four will find it hard to cope with the Five's impulsiveness and constant desire for change and movement. The Five, on the other hand, will not put up with the Four's sober habits and will display fierce resentment toward the Four's attempts to restrict their movements. Arguments regarding finances are certain to arise.

A successful business partnership can be formed with the Fours in charge of finances and production and the Fives taking over communication and selling.

## Four and Six

This is a splendid combination in business as well as in private life. Finances will be safe in the hands of either party. Neither party will be inclined to take a gamble. Common sense and logic will be the governing factors in all their dealings. In personal relationships, their common love of home will hold them together. Both parties will be fond of the culinary arts and share the love of ease and other physical comforts. Their homes will vibrate with simplicity, hospitality, and harmony.

## Four and Seven

A lasting association of any sort is assured with this pair. Each one will show high regard for the other's desire for perfection in whatever activity they engage in—the Four particularly in mechanics and technology, the Seven in scientific and other intellectual pursuits. Their common ground will be love of the land. Financial stability is assured, since both parties have an excellent money sense. The Four's practicality will combine well with the Seven's imagination and insight. Their family lives will be secure and harmonious.

More lightheartedness should be brought into this union. The stronger Four may not always agree with the Seven in their research into the metaphysical aspects of life, though they will respect the Seven's need for fulfillment in this area.

## Four and Eight

This is one of the strongest possible partnerships in business. Both parties are commercially oriented—the Four toward small to average-size businesses and the Eight toward enterprises on a large scale. The combining of these two will lift the Four nearer the limitless ambitions of the Eight, thus forming a powerful and resourceful partnership. The Four will continue to look after the practical day-to-day responsibilities, while the Eight will use their entrepreneurial skills to constantly seek the expansion of their undertakings.

Harmony will exist in private life as well. Both partners have the same ambitions, albeit on different levels. Almost immediate success in the material world will be the reward of their efforts, and they will always have a healthy bank balance. However, both parties are likely to expose themselves to the danger of overwork.

## Four and Nine

As these are different types with well-established personalities of their own, one can learn a great deal from the other. The greatest gifts of the Four, which the Nine lack, are common sense, practicality, emotional stability, and financial acumen. The Four, in turn, can be introduced to the wide world of travel and cultural activity under the influence of the Nine. The Four will need to cooperate and not try to curtail the many outside interests of the Nine. They may support the Nine behind the scenes or join them in the foreground of activity. Either way, the Four will benefit. The Nine will not be without gain either. If these adjustments are made through the practicality of the Four and the wisdom of the Nine, an outstanding association can be established.

## Four and Eleven

In a long-term personal relationship, many adjustments will be required. The Four will consider the Eleven merely a talker and a dreamer. The pragmatic Four will find it difficult to adjust to the idealism of the Eleven. The Eleven will experience extreme restlessness and constriction under the discipline of the Four. Yet in business, they could profit by the wise use of each other's talents. The inventive genius of the Eleven could be put to practical use and physical form by the Four.

## Four and Twenty-Two

The internationalism and unlimited range of the outlook of the Twenty-two may be a bit too much for the conservative Four. There may be upsets in private life. The Four's natural desire to settle down into a secure niche will not be fulfilled by the impersonal and active Twenty-two. A business association could be much easier. The Twenty-two will need and come to depend on the loyalty and reliability of the Four.

## *Five*

## Five and One

*See One and Five on page 185.*

## Five and Two

*See Two and Five on page 189.*

## Five and Three

*See Three and Five on page 192.*

## Five and Four

*See Four and Five on page 196.*

## Five and Five

This creates a relationship in which close bonds will not be maintained. There will be no restraint on each other's freedom of movement. One will not attempt to pry into the other's life. Rare attempts to do so will result in dishonesty by both parties. The combination of these two impetuous types will lead to strife. Their domestic lives will be in disorder and so will the state of their finances. Both will enjoy a streak of luck in gambling, but money is likely to go out faster than it comes in. One party will constantly attempt to shift the responsibility of mundane duties onto the other. Either separately or together, they will be constantly on the move. Although considerable initial excitement will be enjoyed, the association will inevitably come to an early termination.

## Five and Six

In domestic life, a great deal of hard work will be required for a meaningful relationship to be achieved between the Five and the Six. The Five's restlessness and impulsiveness will constantly clash with the Six's attachment to home and domestic responsibilities. The Five may often leave the Six carrying the weight of those responsibilities alone. The Five's frequent absence from home will generate the Six's suspicion and jealousy. The Five will not be able to cope with the restrictions the Six will attempt to impose on them. If the Five can contain their restlessness and accept their share of domestic responsibility, this pair can join in and enjoy much social activity. In business life, many of these problems will not arise and a profitable association can be formed.

## Five and Seven

In private life, this partnership will be incompatible. The tension and intense activity of the Five will upset the Seven's search for quietude and privacy. The natural curiosity of the Five will make troublesome inroads into the Seven's love of privacy. The Five will feel left out of the Seven's company, and their hurried attempts to gain entry into the contemplative world of the Seven will only drive the latter further into themselves. The Five will not be able to respect the needs of the Seven. The Seven for their part will find the Five much too noisy, emotional, and unreliable. They will, however, appreciate the Five's versatility and alert and active minds and tolerate them up to a point. They can become good friends and acquaintances because the Five's high spirits will lift the Seven out of their customary seriousness.

Mutual respect for each other's intelligence and expertise in their own areas will make this a good business partnership—the Five being the front person and the Seven active in the background.

## Five and Eight

This combination proves a difficult one in personal relationships. Emotional control will be a grave problem. Also, one will try to run the life of the other. The Five will find the Eight too conservative, while the Eight will charge the Five with irresponsibility. If the two meet each other halfway, a profitable relationship can be formed. The versatility of the Five will be of inestimable value to the schemes of the Eight. The judgment of the Eight will act as a buffer to the impetuosness of the Five.

This can be turned into a lucrative business association, with the Eight building and producing and the Five buying and selling. Domestic life will be a low priority. The little time left after business affairs will be spent on travel and social obligations.

## Five and Nine

This makes a happy combination. Both parties have open minds and are able to adjust to changing circumstances without effort. Love of travel and a natural curiosity will be a strong common bond. Once again the Five's great versatility will be of real help to the idealistic and impractical Nine. The Nine's wisdom will guide the volatile Five. This pair can gather an enormous amount of experience in life. They will not be without friction, however. Both are emotional, with the Five constantly displaying their emotions and the Nine bottling them up and erupting from time to time.

This is not a strong business combination. Neither party is really business-minded. Human relationships and worldly experience are more important. The domestic side of life will, on the other hand, be of little importance. Very little time will be spent at home.

## Five and Eleven

This is an unproductive combination. There will be much talk and little performance. They will enjoy each other's company and exchange ideas freely. The Five, who has a much greater need for physical experience, will find the Eleven rather high-minded, while the Eleven will accuse the Five of immaturity.

## Five and Twenty-Two

The versatility of the Five will once again be harnessed by the practical Twenty-two, especially in business. In private life, the mature Twenty-two will find the attitudes of the Five somewhat juvenile. The Five will need to submit to the superior wisdom of the Twenty-two.

## *Six*

### Six and One

*See One and Six on page 186.*

### Six and Two

*See Two and Six on page 189.*

### Six and Three

*See Three and Six on page 193.*

### Six and Four

*See Four and Six on page 197.*

### Six and Five

*See Five and Six on page 200.*

### Six and Six

This will be a partnership of deep tranquility, with home as the center of all activity. These partners will experience much happiness in jointly beautifying their homes, spending much time in them, and participating in innumerable common interests. No form of competition will enter here. A life of comfort, enjoyed at an easy pace, will be preferred to the competitive rat race to satisfy high ambitions. These people will be well known for their old-fashioned hospitality; however, those who need a faster and more exciting form of entertainment will find the Six somewhat dull. A business association will show lack of enterprise and the absence of a strong competitive spirit.

## Six and Seven

Both partners are home based, though the home may be a place of accord as well as discord. The Six's natural hospitality and customary use of the home for entertainment will not be shared by the Seven, who will prefer their home to be a sanctuary for privacy. Home maintenance will not cause problems, since the Six will have full run of the house while the Seven will take charge of the garden. The Six's need for conversation will not be met by the taciturn Seven. Both parties are subject to forms of melancholy. The Six's desire for social service will not be shared by the reclusive Seven.

Despite these apparent basic differences, a very meaningful and lasting partnership can be established if these people understand each other's genuine needs. The Seven will meet the Six's spiritual needs, while the Seven will find that all domestic chores will be looked after by their Six partners.

They do make a good business combination. Success will be achieved through sound financial knowledge and a reputation for honesty and responsibility.

## Six and Eight

This creates one of the strongest combinations in the domestic scene. The Six will provide all the support in the home, while the Eight builds a career in business or public service. There will be no competition here, as each will support the other. Their homes will be showpieces of affluence. The community will also benefit from this type of partnership through the social service of the Six and the philanthropy of the Eight.

Business associations will be equally successful.

## Six and Nine

A natural attraction exists between these people, promising a most compatible union in personal life. A deep and abiding friendship will automatically develop. There will be agreement in almost all aspects of living; their aims will be the same. Selfishness will not enter here. Each one will bring out the best in the other. Both parties are humanitarians, dedicated to selfless service, from which a great deal of happiness will be derived. They will also be jointly dedicated to the pursuit of a genteel and refined way of life.

There will be no lack of support for each other in business life either. However, neither party will be especially business minded. Businesses dealing with the relief of human suffering will attract these people.

## Six and Eleven

This creates a good combination. Both parties are idealists and will be able to communicate on a mental level and satisfy each other's need for oral expression. Both are dedicated to a peaceful way of life, though the Eleven can be spirited and explosive when they allow themselves to be carried away by their inspirations. The Six will see that the domestic responsibilities are not neglected, while the Eleven will offer wider perspectives and greater opportunities for motivation. This also creates a good business partnership. The Six's excellent money sense and the Eleven's inventiveness can work successfully together.

## Six and Twenty-Two

This is an association where harmony will prevail, provided the Six is prepared to assume the greater portion of domestic responsibilities and allow the Twenty-two freedom of action. Common ground will be found in humanitarian works and social involvement. It also creates a good business arrangement. Mutual trust, responsibility, and honesty will contribute to form a strong association.

# Seven

## Seven and One

*See One and Seven on page 186.*

## Seven and Two

*See Two and Seven on page 189.*

## Seven and Three

*See Three and Seven on page 193.*

## Seven and Four

*See Four and Seven on page 197.*

## Seven and Five

*See Five and Seven on page 201.*

## Seven and Six

*See Six and Seven on page 204.*

## Seven and Seven

Many unusual features will arise from this combination. Each will be intuitively aware of the other's needs. Very little oral communication will take place, nor will there be demonstration of emotion. A strong bond will be forged through their mutual interest in study, love of nature, and a somewhat reclusive way of life. They will be oblivious to the common issues that normally absorb the attention of the average person. The pair will soon gain a reputation for unapproachability. Pettiness will not enter this relationship. Both parties may suffer from dreaminess and melancholy, the latter being brought about by frustration because of pressures from the outside world. They will be content to live in an inner world of their own and will always resent and reject any intrusions.

This pairing also creates a good business combination, provided that selling goods and public relations are not involved.

## Seven and Eight

A business partnership of considerable profit and strength can be formed between these two. The Seven's natural flair for wise investments and other money dealings will combine well with the Eight's business and executive talents. The Eight will find the Seven scrupulously honest and entirely dependable, while the Seven will be more than content to work within the business network built up by the Eight. Personal relationships will be difficult. The spiritually oriented Seven, who can detach from their material possessions, will not be happy with the worldly Eight, whose measure of success is determined by power and wealth.

The Seven's aloofness will upset the Eight, who will expect support and cooperation in their affairs. The pair will find it difficult to meet on common ground. The Eight will need to respect the Seven's need for seclusion and individuality, and any attempts to organize the lives of the Seven will only drive the latter further into themselves.

The assertive habits adopted by the Eight in business should not be used in the domestic scene.

## Seven and Nine

A relationship of great fulfillment can be developed here, once the natural tendencies of each party are understood and accepted. Their common ground will be the accumulation of worthwhile knowledge and spiritual unfolding, and no closer bond can exist than this joint venture into the realms of metaphysics. However, the Seven will want to remain within these realms of inquiry with no desire to transform their knowledge into the world of activity, while the Nine will feel the urge to preach and find practical ways to apply the knowledge and wisdom they have gained. Reconciliation is needed between these two attitudes.

On a day-to-day level, the soft-spoken and aloof Seven will accept the Nine's ability to communicate ideas. More importantly, the Seven, who is the most intolerant of all loud and abrasive individuals, will respect the superior quality of the Nine's speech and well-informed mind.

## Seven and Eleven

The Seven will agree with much of the idealism of the Eleven but will not go beyond mental acceptance. They will not be seen with the Eleven on the same platform. The methods of the Eleven will not be to their liking. The Seven is able to see through the impracticality of many of the Eleven's schemes. However, when the Eleven functions on a scientific level, they will find support from the Seven. Common ground is found here. The Eleven should take care not to talk excessively with their Seven partners.

## Seven and Twenty-Two

The Seven may find it tiresome to keep up with the many activities of the Twenty-two. They will resent demands made on their time, especially if public appearances are involved. If this problem is overcome, mutual respect for each other's spiritual awareness, combined with practicality, will hold them together in a worthwhile relationship.

# *Eight*

## Eight and One

*See One and Eight on page 186.*

## Eight and Two

*See Two and Eight on page 190.*

## Eight and Three

*See Three and Eight on page 194.*

## Eight and Four

*See Four and Eight on page 197.*

## Eight and Five

*See Five and Eight on page 201.*

## Eight and Six

*See Six and Eight on page 204.*

## Eight and Seven

*See Seven and Eight on page 207.*

## Eight and Eight

Mutual recognition of each other's talents and the resulting coalition of power will make this a formidable partnership in business. It is this type of combination that is able to sweep aside all forms of competition.

In personal affairs, the situation may be complicated. Without the common aim of business success, two authoritative and organized people will want to gain ascendency over each other. This contest will be unconscious, and if its futility is recognized at the early stages and a policy of cooperation adopted, another powerful union can be formed. Both parties are sensitive and their feelings are easily hurt. Emotional turmoil will do much damage to an intimate relationship, and this too must be closely watched.

## Eight and Nine

This pairing creates a good business combination. The wider perspectives of the Nine will enhance the high ambitions of the Eight. The invaluable asset of the Nine's ambassadorial talents will be put to maximum use.

In private life, the Eight will seek to control the Nine. The Eight will not be pleased with the Nine's generosity, impressionability, and unprofessional way. The Nine, on the other hand, will begrudge the amount of time the Eight spends at work. Also, the Eight's lack of interest in social, cultural, and spiritual matters will disturb the Nine. However, the Eight's high sense of justice and the Nine's wisdom can combine to overcome these basic differences. If both parties work toward the success of their relationship, accomplishment rather than failure will be the result.

## Eight and Eleven

The Eight controls the running of a business and can make practical and profitable use of the Eleven's inventive and inspirational side. In domestic life and other personal relationships, the Eight will be intolerant toward the Eleven's impracticality, idealism, and indifference to financial gain. The Eleven will naturally resent what they will regard as materialistic attitudes in the Eight and their lack of interest in abstract matters.

## Eight and Twenty-Two

An association here can turn out to be outstanding in both business and personal life. A few personality problems will have to be overcome, however, before success is achieved. The superior Twenty-two will have the capacity to make the correct overtures and handle the assertive Eight. The Eight, in turn, will not fail to respect the exceptional talents of their Twenty-two associates and loved ones.

# *Nine*

## Nine and One

*See One and Nine on page 187.*

## Nine and Two

*See Two and Nine on page 190.*

## Nine and Three

*See Three and Nine on page 194.*

## Nine and Four

*See Four and Nine on page 198.*

## Nine and Five

*See Five and Nine on page 202.*

## Nine and Six

*See Six and Nine on page 205.*

## Nine and Seven

*See Seven and Nine on page 208.*

## Nine and Eight

*See Eight and Nine on page 211.*

## Nine and Nine

Two Nines can form an association that provides unlimited scope for the expression of wide-ranging interests in human relations. Coexistence will be easy and enriched by mutual cooperation in all their joint ventures. There will, however, be an occasional outburst of anger leading to critical exchange of words between the two. These outbursts will usually be brief and will not damage the relationship. Association on a personal level will be more profitable than on a business level, though the two can combine well in administration and organization at executive levels in government service and large business concerns.

## Nine and Eleven

The visionary outlook of these parties may bring them together but not necessarily hold them together, unless they try to be more practical and down-to-earth. Too much idealism and too little practicality will be the problem here. The domestic side of life will be neglected. A successful business partnership is unlikely, since neither party will be interested in buying, selling, and other aspects of commercial and industrial life.

## Nine and Twenty-Two

A good business association can be formed from this combination, with the Twenty-two bringing practical application into the partnership. The Nine will provide expertise in public relations. In family life, the down-to-earth Twenty-two may find the mentally oriented Nine overly generous and restless. In spite of these differences, an association of considerable benefit to themselves and many others can be formed without much difficulty.

## *Eleven*

## Eleven and One

*See One and Eleven on page 187.*

## Eleven and Two

*See Two and Eleven on page 190.*

## Eleven and Three

*See Three and Eleven on page 195.*

## Eleven and Four

*See Four and Eleven on page 198.*

## Eleven and Five

*See Five and Eleven on page 202.*

## Eleven and Six

*See Six and Eleven on page 205.*

## Eleven and Seven

*See Seven and Eleven on page 209.*

## Eleven and Eight

*See Eight and Eleven on page 211.*

## Eleven and Nine

*See Nine and Eleven on page 214.*

## Eleven and Eleven

This is a lively combination that will be full of mutual interest in abstract thought. A constant exchange of ideas will take place. The inventiveness of the Elevens, if brought out and combined, will see an association of great productivity.

## Eleven and Twenty-Two

This combination is a most desirable association in both business and personal affairs. One will complement the other perfectly. The inventiveness, idealism, and power of speech of the Eleven will merge easily with the practicality and humanitarianism of the Twenty-two.

# *Twenty-Two*

## Twenty-Two and One

*See One and Twenty-Two on page 187.*

## Twenty-Two and Two

*See Two and Twenty-Two on page 191.*

## Twenty-Two and Three

*See Three and Twenty-Two on page 195.*

## Twenty-Two and Four

*See Four and Twenty-Two on page 199.*

## Twenty-Two and Five

*See Five and Twenty-Two on page 202.*

## Twenty-Two and Six

*See Six and Twenty-Two on page 206.*

## Twenty-Two and Seven

*See Seven and Twenty-Two on page 209.*

## Twenty-Two and Eight

*See Eight and Twenty-Two on page 212.*

## Twenty-Two and Nine

*See Nine and Twenty-Two on page 214.*

## Twenty-Two and Eleven

*See Eleven and Twenty-Two on page 216.*

## Twenty-Two and Twenty-Two

This is a rarely found combination. The merger of these two very powerful people could lead to competition, resulting either in frustration or a coalition of power that leads to unlimited potential for enterprise.

> *Do not believe anything on hearsay. Do not believe any traditions that are old and handed down through many generations. Do not believe anything on account of rumors or because people talk much about it. Do not believe simply because the written testament of some ancient sage has shown thee. Never believe anything because presumption is in its favor, or because the custom of years leads thee to regard it as truth. Do not believe anything on the mere authority of teachers or priests. Whatever according to thine own experience and after thorough investigation agrees with thy reason and is conducive to thy well-being and that of all other living creatures, that accept as true accordingly.*
>
> —GAUTAMA BUDDHA

# APPENDIX 1

## SPHERES OF INFLUENCE CHART

The Six Spheres of Influence utilize an individual's birthdate and name to calculate six key areas that govern the personality, destiny, talents, expression, inner person, and outer person. The following chart summarizes each sphere with its prime characteristics and sample calculations.

| Sphere | Calculated with | Indicates | Example | Page reference |
|---|---|---|---|---|
| **First Sphere:** Sphere of Personality | The day of birth | Kind of personality, and establishes individuality—most important Sphere | $12/20/1983 \rightarrow 2+0 = 2$<br><br>$2$ is the vibration of the First Sphere | 3, 13<br>Master Numbers: 2, 71 |
| **Second Sphere:** Sphere of Destiny | The sum of the entire birthdate (month, day, and year) | How the personality is drawn toward a Life Path influence by the vibration of this Sphere | $12/20/1983 \rightarrow 1+2+2+0+1+9+8+3 = 26$<br>$\rightarrow 2+6 = 8$<br><br>$8$ is the vibration of the Second Sphere | 4, 81<br>Master Numbers: 2, 71 |
| **Third Sphere:** Sphere of the Given Name | The given/first name or nickname | Personality and talents | $JARROD \rightarrow 1+1+9+9+6+4 = 30 \rightarrow 3+0 = 3$<br><br>$3$ is the vibration of the Third Sphere | 6, 101; alphabet chart: 6 |
| **Fourth Sphere:** Sphere of Expression | The whole name (first, middle, and last) | Further talents as well as a channel through which they can be expressed (e.g., career) | $JARROD \rightarrow 1+1+9+9+6+4 = 30 \rightarrow 3+0 = 3$<br>$LEE \rightarrow 3+5+5 = 13 \rightarrow 1+3 = 4$<br>$ANDERSON \rightarrow 1+5+4+5+9+1+6+5 = 36$<br>$\rightarrow 3+6 = 9 \longrightarrow 3+4+9 = 16 \rightarrow 1+6 = 7$<br><br>$7$ is the vibration of the Fourth Sphere | 7, 129; alphabet chart: 6, 221 |
| **Fifth Sphere:** Sphere of the Inner Person | The vowels within the whole name | The inner person | $JARROD \rightarrow 1+6 = 7$<br>$LEE \rightarrow 5+5 = 10 \rightarrow 1+0 = 1$<br>$ANDERSON \rightarrow 1+5+6 = 12 \rightarrow 1+2 = 3$<br>$7+1+3 = 11 \rightarrow 1+1 = 2$<br><br>$2$ is the vibration of the Fifth Sphere | 8, 145; alphabet chart: 6, 221<br>Y as vowel: 8 |
| **Sixth Sphere:** Sphere of the Outer Person | The consonants within the whole name | The outer person | $JARROD \rightarrow 1+9+9+4 = 23 \rightarrow 2+3 = 5$<br>$LEE \rightarrow 3$<br>$ANDERSON \rightarrow 5+4+9+1+5 = 24$<br>$\rightarrow 2+4 = 6$<br>$5+3+6 = 14 \rightarrow 1+4 = 5$<br><br>$5$ is the vibration of the Sixth Sphere | 9, 161; alphabet chart: 6, 221<br>Y as vowel: 8 |

# APPENDIX 2

---

# NUMERIC LETTER VALUES CHART

This chart gives the number value of all the letters in the alphabet, which are used to calculate the Third, Fourth, Fifth, and Sixth Spheres (see pages 5–9) as well as the Birth and Name Grids (see chapter 5 and the examples on pages 120–127).

| 1 | 2 | 3 | 4 | 5 | 6 | 7 | 8 | 9 |
|---|---|---|---|---|---|---|---|---|
| A | B | C | D | E | F | G | H | I |
| J | K | L | M | N | O | P | Q | R |
| S | T | U | V | W | X | Y | Z |   |

# APPENDIX 3

## OVERVIEW OF THE GRIDS

### Fixed Grid

**The Fixed Grid** is the template used to calculate an individual's Birth and Name Grids (see page 120 and 121 as well as the sections that follow in this appendix). It shows the fixed position of the numerals 1 through 9 on horizontal and vertical planes. The horizontal planes, for example, indicate levels of expression—Mental, Emotional, and Physical (from top to bottom). The vertical planes indicate an individual's attitude toward self and others—primarily on a mental and/or intuitional level. Use the table below as well as the information in chapter 2 (pages 13–79) to determine the influence/tendency of these numbers within the grid (i.e., the number 8 has an emotional influence on personal expression and a mental angle when it comes to assessing the self and others).

| | | | |
|---|---|---|---|
| *3* | *6* | *9* | **Mental Plane** |
| *2* | *5* | *8* | **Emotional Plane** |
| *1* | *4* | *7* | **Physical Plane** |

Self    Community    Global

**(Consciousness)**

Number 1   Physical/Mental

Number 2   Emotional/Intuitional

Number 3   Mental/Emotional

Number 4   Physical

Number 5   Emotional/Physical/
                 Mental/Intuitional

Number 6   Mental

Number 7   Physical/Intuitional

Number 8   Emotional/Mental

Number 9   Mental/Intuitional/
                 Emotional

# Birth Grid

**The Birth Grid** is created by using the numerals of an individual's birthdate (month, day, year). Referring to the Fixed Grid for number positions, fill in only the relevant numbers within the grid. Underline the First Sphere number (birth day—see page 3) and double underline the Second Sphere number (the sum of the birthdate [month, day, year]—see page 4). Remember, the Zero does not contribute attributes of its own, so including it in the grid is optional (sometimes it is visually helpful to do so). If you do include it, put it in the same position as the 1. See the example below as well as pages 110 and 123.

# JARROD LEE ANDERSON

## *12/20/1983*

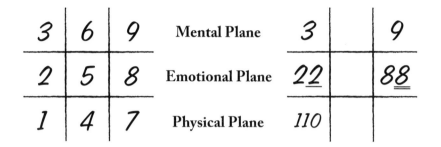

| | | | Plane | | | |
|---|---|---|---|---|---|---|
| 3 | 6 | 9 | Mental Plane | 3 | | 9 |
| 2 | 5 | 8 | Emotional Plane | 2<u>2</u> | | <u>88</u> |
| 1 | 4 | 7 | Physical Plane | 110 | | |

- First Sphere (one underline): 2 (from 20, the birth day)
- Second Sphere (two underlines): 8 (1 + 2 + 2 + 0 + 1 + 9 + 8 + 3 = 26 = 8)
- Expression and Attitude: Based on the position of the numbers in the grid, Jarrod is mostly influenced by emotions and mental input, though intuition and physical responses also affect him.

## Name Grid

**The Name Grid** differs from the Fixed Grid and Birth Grid in that it shows how many times the numeric values of the full name appear in their fixed positions in the grid. (These can add to, balance, and sometimes counteract the numeric influences of the Birth Grid.) Calculate the numeric value of each letter of the whole name by using the Numeric Values Chart (Appendix 2, page 221) and the method demonstrated below. Then enter the numbers' frequency into the grid according to their Fixed Grid positions. (See also pages 120 and 121 for more information.) For example, in the case of Jarrod Lee Anderson, you will have four 1s, one 3, two 4s, five 5s, two 6s, and three 9s.

## *JARROD LEE ANDERSON*

*119964 355 15459165*

Number of times vibrations appear in the whole name:

| Vibration | Quantity of Letters |
|:---:|:---:|
| 1 | 4 |
| 2 | 0 |
| 3 | 1 |
| 4 | 2 |
| 5 | 5 |
| 6 | 2 |
| 7 | 0 |
| 8 | 0 |
| 9 | 3 |

**FIXED GRID**                                    **NAME GRID**

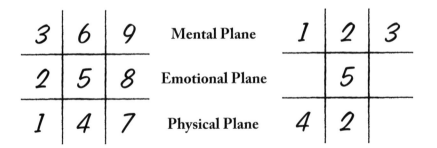

| 3 | 6 | 9 | Mental Plane | 1 | 2 | 3 |
|---|---|---|---|---|---|---|
| 2 | 5 | 8 | Emotional Plane | | 5 | |
| 1 | 4 | 7 | Physical Plane | 4 | 2 | |

If you wish to review the full interpretation of Jarrod's Name Grid, please refer to pages 171–172.

# APPENDIX 4

## VOWEL RULES

The vowels of the whole name (first, middle, and last) show the most subtle aspects of the personality—the inner person, or the person not generally presented to the world—when their numeric values are added together to determine a person's Fifth Sphere. (Please refer to pages 8 and 9 for more information on the Fifth Sphere.)

The vowels *A*, *E*, *I*, *O*, and *U* convert directly to 1, 5, 9, 6, and 3, respectively, in accordance with the Numeric Letter Values chart (see page 6). The letter *Y*, which converts to 7, is counted as a vowel if it is found in a position where it functions as a vowel, as in the following instances:

1. When there is no other vowel in the name, as in Flynn or Lynn
2. When there is no vowel in the syllable, as in Tyrone or Sylvia
3. When it is preceded by another vowel and sounded as one, as in Guy or Jayne

# APPENDIX 5

## EXAMPLES OF SPHERE CALCULATIONS

### Emily Kay Mitchell: February 9, 2006 (2/9/2006)

#### *The First Sphere of Influence*

The Sphere of Personality is derived from the number or numbers of the day of birth.

*2 / 9 / 2006*   ⟶   *9*

**Vibration 9 Personality Sketch**

A prominent feature of this birthdate is the absence of a physical vibration and the predominance of emotional outlets, because although the 9 vibration of the birthday belongs to the mental realm, it does contain a good deal of emotional expression. Combined with the fluid 2 vibrations in her birth month and year, Emily has a degree of emotionality that may often create adverse actions and reactions. A physical vibration is needed to help her exercise control over her emotions. If not, she may suffer from mood changes, aloofness, indecision, and inadequacy in self-confidence and self-reliance.

## The Second Sphere of Influence

The Sphere of Destiny is derived from the birthdate totaled and reduced to a single digit.

*2 / 9 / 2006     2 + 9 + 2 + 0 + 0 + 6 = 19* ⟶ *1 + 9 = 10* ⟶ *1 + 0 = 1*

### Vibration 1 Destiny Sketch

All is not lost, so to speak. Emily need not continue fighting against any possible negative tendencies caused by an excess of emotion, because her Destiny is a much-needed physical 1 vibration. It will exercise a pull in the direction of self-control, self-worth, direction, and an authoritative display of several outstanding attributes of her 9 and 2.

However, it will also become necessary for her, through self-study, to become aware of this condition and make maximum use of it. The more she gains faith in herself, the sooner she will emerge into her wide world of opportunity.

## The Third Sphere of Influence

The Sphere of the Given Name is totaled and reduced to a single digit.

A better name could not have been chosen. The name Emily, with its 1 vibration, reinforces her Second Sphere of Influence. There will be little doubt that she can overcome any negative tendencies created by the absence of a down-to-earth physical force in her birthdate.

```
1  2  3  4  5  6  7  8  9
A  B  C  D  E  F  G  H  I
J  K  L  M  N  O  P  Q  R
S  T  U  V  W  X  Y  Z
```

**EMILY**
$5 + 4 + 9 + 3 + 7 = 28$    →    $2 + 8 = 10$    →    $1 + 0 = 1$

## The Fourth Sphere of Influence

The Sphere of Expression is derived from the whole name totaled and reduced to a single digit. (Please refer to the numeric values chart in the example above.)

**EMILY**
$5 + 4 + 9 + 3 + 7 = 28$    →    $2 + 8 = 10$    →    $1 + 0 = 1$

**KAY**
$2 + 1 + 7 = 10$    →    $1 + 0 = 1$        $1 + 1 + 1 = 3$

**MITCHELL**
$4 + 9 + 2 + 3 + 8 + 5 + 3 + 3 = 37$    →    $3 + 7 = 10$    →    $1 + 0 = 1$

The 3 vibration in this location brightens and intensifies Emily's mental orientation and aesthetic attributes and also sharpens her sense of accuracy, sense of humor, and quality of speech. It is also in harmony with the 6 and 9 aspects of her birthdate.

## *The Fifth Sphere of Influence*

The Sphere of the Inner Person is derived from the vowels of the whole name totaled and reduced to a single digit. As the *Y* in the second name Kay is next to a vowel it is treated as a vowel (refer to page 8). (Please refer to the numeric values chart on page 221.)

EM*I*LY
$5 + 9 = 14$ → $1 + 4 = 5$

K*A*Y
$1 + 7 = 8$

$5 + 8 + 5 = 18$ → $1 + 8 = 9$

M*I*TCH*E*LL
$9 + 5 = 14$ → $1 + 4 = 5$

In the Fifth Sphere, a characteristic not mentioned in Emily's First Sphere is a global and humanitarian outlook on life. This is a cardinal quality of the 9 vibration. As her inner desires of her Fifth Sphere are also governed by this vibration, she will make a concerted effort to manifest these desires, using the effective forces of her Second, Third, and Fourth Spheres.

## *The Sixth Sphere of Influence*

The Sphere of the Outer Person is derived from the consonants of the whole name totaled and reduced to a single digit. (Please refer to the numeric values chart on page 221.)

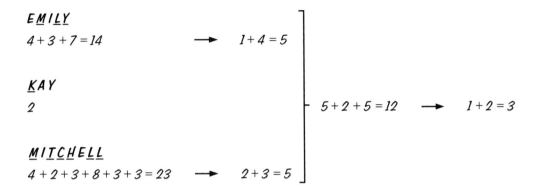

E M I L Y

$4 + 3 + 7 = 14$ $\longrightarrow$ $1 + 4 = 5$

K A Y

$2$

$5 + 2 + 5 = 12$ $\longrightarrow$ $1 + 2 = 3$

M I T C H E L L

$4 + 2 + 3 + 8 + 3 + 3 = 23$ $\longrightarrow$ $2 + 3 = 5$

This vibration in the Sixth Sphere is the same as her Fourth Sphere. Despite moments of self-doubt, which will not be displayed to others, Emily will come across as a happy, friendly, and sociable person. This sphere will also work in conjunction with the outgoing attributes of her First and Fifth Spheres. She will be regarded as a people person.

**FIXED GRID**                **BIRTH GRID**

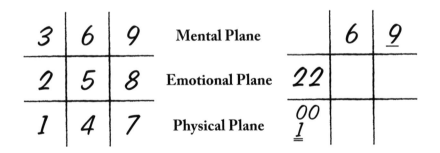

| FIXED GRID | | | | BIRTH GRID | | |
|---|---|---|---|---|---|---|
| 3 | 6 | 9 | Mental Plane | | 6 | 9 |
| 2 | 5 | 8 | Emotional Plane | 22 | | |
| 1 | 4 | 7 | Physical Plane | 00 1 | | |

# Robert Daniel Lopez: April 22, 1999 (4/22/1999)

## *The First Sphere of Influence*

The Sphere of Personality is derived from the number or numbers of the day of birth.

*4/22/1999*  ⟶  *22*

As a Master Vibration, 22 isn't reduced further (see page 2 for more information).

### Vibration 22 Personality Sketch

Because 22 is a Master Vibration, it can be a complex birthday to assess. Therefore, it is necessary to also take into serious consideration the qualities of the 4 (2 + 2 = 4).

To assume that all persons born on the 22nd will function and reach the comprehensive heights of the 22 vibration is inaccurate; if they are fortunate enough to do so, a good deal will depend upon the vibration of the birth month, prevailing conditions, and opportunities and other extraneous forces that influence the personality. The best we can do is keep in mind the high potential of this force and assess the personality as a powerful Four with the 22 characteristics taken into consideration, as no doubt, certain powers of the Master vibration will emerge from time to time.

In Robert's case, it is likely that positive and negative features of the 4 may express themselves in equal proportion. This is due to the repetition of the 4 vibration in the birthday and birth month. Some negative features produced by this combination will be an absence of sentiment, especially toward the feelings of others, excess of discipline, petty-mindedness, stubbornness, selfishness, especially in money matters, and a constant drive for power and material possessions. On the positive side, Robert will possess an excellent business sense, money management skills, innumerable practical skills, physical endurance, and the ability to overcome any personal handicaps.

## The Second Sphere of Influence

The Sphere of Destiny is derived from the birthdate totaled and reduced to a single digit.

$4/22/1999 \quad 4 + 2 + 2 + 1 + 9 + 9 + 9 = 36 \quad \longrightarrow \quad 3 + 6 = 9$

### Vibration 9 Personality Sketch

The 9 destiny is most fortunate in this case, as it can lift Robert out of his entrenched physical and material lifestyle created by the combined 22/4 of his birthday and the 4 of his birth month into wider perspectives. With the 9 interacting in this sphere, Robert has a much better chance of fulfilling some of the high potential of his Master Vibration. An inspirational, generous, and unbiased global outlook is just what he needs; however, this will not be any easy task and may take some time.

## The Third Sphere of Influence

The Sphere of the Given Name is totaled and reduced to a single digit by using the numeric values chart below.

| 1 | 2 | 3 | 4 | 5 | 6 | 7 | 8 | 9 |
|---|---|---|---|---|---|---|---|---|
| A | B | C | D | E | F | G | H | I |
| J | K | L | M | N | O | P | Q | R |
| S | T | U | V | W | X | Y | Z | |

*ROBERT*

*9 + 6 + 2 + 5 + 9 + 2 = 33*  →  *3 + 3 = 6*

Robert is an excellent name choice for his birthdate. The Six is a strong force within the mental realm. It represents, among other things, balance, reasoning, and deliberation, and, in Robert's case, it complements and strengthens the First and Second spheres and adds several desirable attributes of the 6 vibration. Most importantly, it adds community consciousness, social service, and domestic responsibility. This name certainly helps with the call of his destiny.

## The Fourth Sphere of Influence

The Sphere of Expression is derived from the whole name totaled and reduced to a single digit. (Please refer to the numeric chart on page 221.)

*ROBERT*

*9 + 6 + 2 + 5 + 9 + 2 = 33*  →  *3 + 3 = 6*

*DANIEL*

*4 + 1 + 5 + 9 + 5 + 3 = 27*  →  *2 + 7 = 9*

*LOPEZ*

*3 + 6 + 7 + 5 + 8 = 29*  →  *2 + 9 = 11*  →  *1 + 1 = 2*

*6 + 9 + 2 = 17*

*1 + 7 = 8*

This is yet another complementary vibration. The 8 in Robert's Fourth Sphere provides authority and administrative and organizational powers essential for positions of authority in government, corporations, or even religious institutions; however, Robert could also be exposed to the danger of exercising excessive discipline and control over subordinates, so it is something he should stay aware of. This may conflict with his understanding and sympathetic requirements of his 9 destiny.

## The Fifth Sphere of Influence

The Sphere of the Inner Person is derived from the vowels of the whole name totaled and reduced to a single digit. (Please refer to the numeric chart on page 221.)

ROBERT
6 + 5 = 11 ⟶ 1 + 1 = 2

DANIEL
1 + 9 + 5 = 15 ⟶ 1 + 5 = 6 ⎫ 2 + 6 + 2 = 10 ⟶ 1 + 0 = 1

LOPEZ
6 + 5 = 11 ⟶ 1 + 1 = 2

The 1 is yet another complementary feature for Robert. This vibration makes him think in terms of leadership, individuality, originality, creativity, and noninterference. These inner thoughts and desires are in keeping with the powers and capacities of the Master Vibration of his birthday—all other Spheres of Influence support these urges as well. He will be frustrated only when outer circumstances and lack of opportunity deprive him of expressing himself as he desires.

## *The Sixth Sphere of Influence*

The Sphere of the Outer Person is derived from the consonants of the whole name totaled and reduced to a single digit. (Please refer to the chart on page 221).

$$R\underline{O}B\underline{E}R\underline{T}$$
$$9 + 2 + 9 + 2 = 22 \longrightarrow 2 + 2 = 4$$

$$D\underline{A}N\underline{IE}L$$
$$4 + 5 + 3 = 12 \longrightarrow 1 + 2 = 3 \quad \left] \quad 4 + 3 + 9 = 16 \longrightarrow 1 + 6 = 7 \right.$$

$$L\underline{O}P\underline{E}Z$$
$$3 + 7 + 8 = 18 \longrightarrow 1 + 8 = 9$$

The 7 in Robert's Sixth Sphere complements the spiritual and humanitarian aspects created by his 22 birthday and the three 9 vibrations that enforce this in his birth year. He will come across not only as a knowledgeable person on mundane matters but also in fields of a philosophical, spiritual, and esoteric nature; however, there is no guarantee that he will explore all of these. His family and social background will affect the degree to which he does so. If he does not explore these fields, he will still project an aura of knowledge in a considerable variety of subjects.

Influenced by the 7 vibration, he will be known as a perennial student, and environmental issues and the study of natural sciences are other areas into which he will be drawn by the combined force of the 22, 9, and 7 aspects of his personality.

## FIXED GRID

## BIRTH GRID

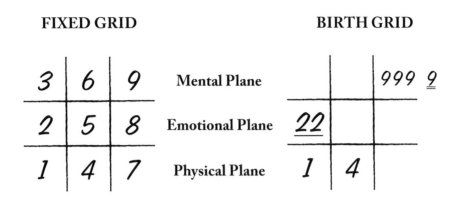

| | | | |
|---|---|---|---|
| 3 | 6 | 9 | Mental Plane |
| 2 | 5 | 8 | Emotional Plane |
| 1 | 4 | 7 | Physical Plane |

# APPENDIX 6

## EXAMPLES OF COMMON CALCULATION ERRORS

Because a false calculation can throw off the resulting interpretation of a person's numbers, do your calculations carefully. Here are a few things to keep in mind:

- Double-check for errors in addition.
- If you are calculating the birthdate and name vibrations of someone else, such as a friend or a celebrity, make sure you have the correct dates and spelling before you proceed.
- Remember that the letter Y may sometimes be found in a position where it functions as a vowel. (Refer to page 8 for more information.)
- Make sure you have read and understood the section on Master Numbers/Vibrations (see page 2).
- Take into account, whenever possible, age and the cultural, religious, social, and economic background of the person you are assessing.

# Common Addition Errors

A common mistake with the Second Sphere is to calculate the single digit of the birthday, month, and year and then add these three numbers together. (See example 1 below.)

## *Example 1*

INCORRECT Second Sphere Calculation:

2/17/1976     $2 + (1 + 7 = 8) + (1 + 9 + 7 + 6 = 23 = 5) = 15 = 6$

CORRECT Second Sphere Calculation:

2/17/1976     $2 + 1 + 7 + 1 + 9 + 7 + 6 = 33 = 6$

Mathematically, the final number will be the same in both calculation methods, but if any Master Numbers are involved, the sphere's true numeric influence could be incorrect. The calculations in the next example demonstrate this.

## *Example 2*

INCORRECT Second Sphere Calculation:

8/15/1961     $8 + (1 + 5 = 6) + (1 + 9 + 6 + 1 = 17 = 8) = 22$

CORRECT Second Sphere Calculation:

8/15/1961     $8 + 1 + 5 + 1 + 9 + 6 + 1 = 31 = 4$

At first, it seems as though the above person has a Master Number dictating his or her destiny, but the reality is a number 4 influence. And remember that Master Numbers only influence the First and Second Spheres. If they appear in the calculation subtotals for the Third, Fourth, Fifth, or Sixth Spheres, they are broken down to a single digit. (For more on Master Numbers/Vibrations, please see pages 2 and 71–78.)

# APPENDIX 7

# GIRL NAMES WITH CORRESPONDING VIBRATIONS

**A**

| | |
|---|---|
| Aaliyah | 3 |
| Abagail | 6 |
| Abbey | 8 |
| Abigail | 5 |
| Ada | 6 |
| Addison | 3 |
| Adel | 4 |
| Adeline | 5 |
| Adelle | 3 |
| Adi | 5 |
| Adriana | 3 |
| Agatha | 2 |
| Agnes | 1 |
| Aida | 6 |
| Aileen | 1 |
| Ailene | 1 |
| Ainslee | 11/2 |
| Ainsley | 4 |
| Akyra | 2 |

| | |
|---|---|
| Alaine | 6 |
| Alana | 11/2 |
| Alayne | 22/4 |
| Alejandra | 3 |
| Alessandra | 4 |
| Alexa | 7 |
| Alexandra | 8 |
| Alexis | 7 |
| Alice | 3 |
| Alicia | 8 |
| Alise | 1 |
| Alisha | 5 |
| Alison | 7 |
| Allegra | 11/2 |
| Allisa | 9 |
| Allison | 1 |
| Ally | 5 |
| Allyson | 8 |
| Alma | 9 |
| Alvinia | 5 |

| | | | |
|---|---|---|---|
| Alyss | 4 | Annette | 7 |
| Alyssa | 5 | Annie | 7 |
| Amalee | 1 | Annika | 5 |
| Amalia | 1 | Annmarie | 3 |
| Amanda | 7 | Antoinetta | 11/2 |
| Amara | 7 | Antoinette | 6 |
| Amber | 3 | Antonia | 11/2 |
| Amelia | 5 | Antonina | 7 |
| Amelie | 9 | Anya | 5 |
| Amie | 1 | April | 11/2 |
| Amy | 3 | Ara | 11/2 |
| Ana | 7 | Arana | 8 |
| Anabel | 8 | Aretha | 8 |
| Anastasia | 22/4 | Ariana | 8 |
| Andi | 1 | Arianna | 4 |
| Andie | 6 | Ariel | 9 |
| Andrea | 7 | Arleen | 1 |
| Andria | 11/2 | Arlene | 1 |
| Anette | 2 | Arlette | 9 |
| Angela | 22/4 | Arlie | 9 |
| Angelica | 7 | Arliene | 1 |
| Angeliene | 9 | Arly | 2 |
| Angelika | 6 | Arlyne | 3 |
| Angelina | 9 | Asha | 11/2 |
| Angelique | 1 | Ashlea | 1 |
| Angie | 9 | Ashlee | 5 |
| Anica | 1 | Ashleigh | 6 |
| Anika | 9 | Ashley | 7 |
| Anita | 9 | Ashlie | 9 |
| Ann | 11/2 | Ashlyn | 7 |
| Anna | 3 | Ashton | 5 |
| Annabel | 22/4 | Astra | 5 |
| Annabelle | 3 | Astred | 22/4 |
| Anne | 7 | Astrid | 8 |
| Annemarie | 8 | Athena | 22/4 |

| | | | |
|---|---|---|---|
| Aubrey | 9 | Bettine | 3 |
| Audra | 9 | Betsy | 8 |
| Audre | 22/4 | Betty | 9 |
| Audrey | 11/2 | Betrix | 6 |
| Audry | 6 | Bev | 11/2 |
| Augusta | 9 | Beverlee | 11/2 |
| Aurelia | 4 | Beverley | 4 |
| Aurora | 11/2 | Beverlie | 6 |
| Autumn | 9 | Beverly | 8 |
| Ava | 6 | Bianca | 3 |
| Avery | 8 | Bianka | 2 |
| | | Billie | 4 |
| **B** | | Blanche | 9 |
| Bailey | 9 | Blyth | 22/4 |
| Barbara | 7 | Blythe | 9 |
| Barbra | 6 | Bo | 8 |
| Bea | 8 | Bobbi | 3 |
| Beatrice | 9 | Bonnie | 5 |
| Beatrix | 7 | Bonny | 7 |
| Belinda | 11/2 | Brandi | 3 |
| Bell | 4 | Brandie | 8 |
| Bella | 5 | Brandy | 1 |
| Belle | 9 | Breanna | 1 |
| Bernadette | 4 | Breanne | 5 |
| Bernadine | 9 | Bree | 3 |
| Bernetta | 4 | Breeanne | 1 |
| Bernice | 11/2 | Brenda | 8 |
| Bertha | 9 | Briana | 9 |
| Beryl | 8 | Brianna | 5 |
| Beryle | 4 | Brianne | 9 |
| Bess | 9 | Bridget | 11/2 |
| Beth | 8 | Brie | 7 |
| Bethany | 3 | Brieanna | 1 |
| Bette | 7 | Briely | 8 |
| Bettina | 8 | Brier | 7 |

| | | | | |
|---|---|---|---|---|
| Brigid | 4 | Carla | 8 |
| Brigit | 11/2 | Carlee | 8 |
| Briony | 11/2 | Carleen | 4 |
| Brit | 4 | Carlen | 8 |
| Britta | 7 | Carlene | 4 |
| Brittany | 1 | Carley | 1 |
| Bronwyn | 3 | Carli | 7 |
| Brooke | 3 | Carlota | 7 |
| Brooklyn | 4 | Carlotta | 9 |
| | | Carly | 5 |
| **C** | | Carmel | 7 |
| Caetlyn | 8 | Carmela | 8 |
| Caitlin | 5 | Carmen | 9 |
| Caitlyn | 3 | Carol | 22/4 |
| Calla | 11/2 | Carolina | 1 |
| Calley | 22/4 | Caroline | 5 |
| Calli | 1 | Carolyn | 7 |
| Cally | 8 | Cass | 6 |
| Camila | 3 | Cassandra | 8 |
| Camilla | 6 | Cassey | 9 |
| Camile | 7 | Cassie | 2 |
| Camille | 1 | Cate | 11/2 |
| Cammi | 3 | Caterina | 8 |
| Cammie | 8 | Catharina | 11/2 |
| Cammy | 1 | Catharine | 7 |
| Candace | 22/4 | Cathee | 6 |
| Candi | 22/4 | Catherina | 7 |
| Candice | 3 | Catherine | 11/2 |
| Candie | 9 | Cathleen | 5 |
| Cara | 5 | Cathlene | 5 |
| Caresa | 2 | Cathryn | 8 |
| Caressa | 3 | Cathy | 3 |
| Cari | 22/4 | Caty | 4 |
| Carin | 9 | Cayley | 8 |
| Carissa | 7 | Cecilia | 6 |

| | | | | |
|---|---|---|---|---|
| Cecily | 3 | | Clarissa | 1 |
| Celeste | 6 | | Clarisse | 5 |
| Celia | 3 | | Claudette | 1 |
| Celina | 8 | | Claudia | 6 |
| Cerise | 5 | | Clea | 3 |
| Chaney | 11/2 | | Clover | 3 |
| Chanel | 7 | | Coco | 9 |
| Chantel | 9 | | Coleen | 9 |
| Chantelle | 8 | | Colleen | 3 |
| Charity | 3 | | Connie | 6 |
| Charleen | 3 | | Constance | 4 |
| Charlene | 3 | | Cora | 1 |
| Charlotte | 3 | | Coralie | 9 |
| Charmaine | 9 | | Coraline | 5 |
| Chastity | 6 | | Cordelia | 4 |
| Chauntel | 3 | | Coretta | 1 |
| Chelsea | 8 | | Corette | 5 |
| Chelsey | 5 | | Corey | 3 |
| Cher | 7 | | Cori | 9 |
| Cheri | 7 | | Cornelia | 5 |
| Cherie | 3 | | Corrie | 5 |
| Cherry | 5 | | Courtney | 4 |
| Cheryl | 8 | | Cristel | 5 |
| Chloe | 7 | | Crystal | 8 |
| Chrissie | 9 | | Cybil | 6 |
| Christel | 4 | | Cynthia | 8 |
| Christina | 11/2 | | | |
| Christine | 6 | | **D** | |
| Chrystal | 7 | | Dahlia | 3 |
| Cindy | 1 | | Daisy | 22/4 |
| Clair | 7 | | Dalia | 9 |
| Claire | 3 | | Dallas | 4 |
| Clara | 8 | | Dana | 11/2 |
| Clare | 3 | | Dani | 1 |
| Clarice | 6 | | Danica | 5 |

| | | | |
|---|---|---|---|
| Daniela | 1 | Dione | 11/2 |
| Danielle | 8 | Dionne | 7 |
| Dannika | 9 | Divine | 1 |
| Daphne | 3 | Dixie | 6 |
| Darby | 5 | Dolly | 5 |
| Darcee | 9 | Dolores | 7 |
| Darcelle | 3 | Dominique | 8 |
| Darleen | 5 | Donna | 3 |
| Darlene | 5 | Dora | 2 |
| Dawn | 6 | Doreen | 7 |
| Deana | 7 | Dorene | 7 |
| Deandra | 11/2 | Doris | 11/2 |
| Deanna | 3 | Dorothea | 5 |
| Deanne | 7 | Dorothy | 6 |
| Debbie | 9 | Dory | 8 |
| Debby | 2 | Dot | 3 |
| Debora | 9 | Dotti | 5 |
| Deborah | 8 | Dottie | 1 |
| Debra | 3 | Dotty | 3 |
| Deidre | 9 | | |
| Delilah | 6 | **E** | |
| Della | 7 | Eartha | 8 |
| Delores | 6 | Ebony | 7 |
| Dena | 6 | Eda | 1 |
| Denise | 11/2 | Edel | 8 |
| Denna | 2 | Eden | 1 |
| Desiree | 11/2 | Edie | 5 |
| Destiny | 6 | Edith | 1 |
| Devon | 6 | Edna | 6 |
| Di | 4 | Edwina | 11/2 |
| Diana | 2 | Edythe | 4 |
| Dianna | 7 | Effie | 4 |
| Dianne | 11/2 | Eileen | 5 |
| Dina | 1 | Elaine | 1 |
| Dinah | 9 | Elana | 6 |

| | | | | |
|---|---|---|---|---|
| Eleanor | 7 | | Estella | 2 |
| Electra | 1 | | Estelle | 6 |
| Elena | 1 | | Esther | 3 |
| Elenore | 11/2 | | Ethel | 5 |
| Elinore | 6 | | Etta | 1 |
| Elisa | 1 | | Ettie | 5 |
| Elisha | 9 | | Etty | 7 |
| Elissa | 2 | | Eugenia | 8 |
| Eliza | 8 | | Eva | 1 |
| Elizabeth | 7 | | Eve | 5 |
| Ella | 3 | | Evelyn | 11/2 |
| Ellen | 3 | | Evie | 5 |
| Ellie | 7 | | Evita | 3 |
| Elly | 9 | | | |
| Ellyn | 5 | | | |
| Eloise | 11/2 | | **F** | |
| Elsa | 1 | | Fae | 3 |
| Elsbeth | 8 | | Faith | 8 |
| Elsie | 5 | | Fallon | 6 |
| Elyse | 3 | | Fanny | 6 |
| Emelda | 4 | | Farrah | 7 |
| Emilia | 4 | | Fatima | 5 |
| Emilie | 8 | | Fawn | 8 |
| Emily | 1 | | Fay | 5 |
| Emma | 5 | | Faye | 1 |
| Emmalisa | 1 | | Fayette | 1 |
| Emmy | 2 | | Felicia | 9 |
| Enid | 5 | | Felicity | 8 |
| Erica | 9 | | Fern | 7 |
| Erika | 8 | | Fiona | 9 |
| Erin | 1 | | Fionna | 5 |
| Erma | 1 | | Flo | 6 |
| Esme | 6 | | Flora | 7 |
| Esmeralda | 6 | | Florence | 6 |
| Essie | 3 | | Fran | 3 |

| | | | | |
|---|---|---|---|---|
| Frances | 3 | Gladys | 5 |
| Francine | 7 | Glenda | 7 |
| Freya | 1 | Gloria | 8 |
| | | Goldie | 7 |
| **G** | | Grace | 7 |
| Gabi | 1 | Gretchen | 8 |
| Gabriel | 9 | Guinevere | 7 |
| Gabriella | 4 | Gwen | 22/4 |
| Gabrielle | 8 | Gwendolyn | 11/2 |
| Gail | 2 | Gwyn | 6 |
| Gayle | 5 | Gwyneth | 3 |
| Gemma | 3 | | |
| Geneva | 9 | **H** | |
| Genesis | 6 | Hailey | 6 |
| Genevieve | 4 | Hanna | 2 |
| Genny | 11/2 | Hannah | 1 |
| Georgette | 3 | Harper | 3 |
| Georgia | 8 | Harriet | 7 |
| Georgianna | 1 | Hattie | 9 |
| Georgie | 3 | Hatty | 2 |
| Georgina | 4 | Haylee | 11/2 |
| Geraldine | 3 | Hayleigh | 3 |
| Geri | 3 | Hayley | 4 |
| Gerri | 3 | Hazel | 7 |
| Gertie | 1 | Heather | 11/2 |
| Gertrude | 8 | Heda | 9 |
| Gianna | 1 | Hedda | 22/4 |
| Gilda | 6 | Heidi | 8 |
| Gillian | 1 | Helen | 8 |
| Gilly | 11/2 | Helena | 9 |
| Gina | 22/4 | Hellene | 11/2 |
| Ginger | 6 | Heloise | 1 |
| Ginny | 6 | Henrietta | 1 |
| Gisele | 3 | Hermione | 6 |
| Giselle | 6 | Hester | 3 |

| | | | | |
|---|---|---|---|---|
| Hilary | 1 | | Ivana | 2 |
| Hilda | 7 | | Ivy | 2 |
| Holli | 11/2 | | | |
| Hollie | 7 | | **J** | |
| Holly | 9 | | Jacinda | 6 |
| Honor | 7 | | Jacki | 7 |
| Hope | 8 | | Jackie | 3 |
| Hortense | 5 | | Jacklin | 6 |
| | | | Jaclyn | 2 |
| **I** | | | Jacqueline | 7 |
| Ida | 5 | | Jacquelyn | 9 |
| Ilana | 1 | | Jade | 11/2 |
| Ileana | 6 | | Jaime | 2 |
| Ilene | 9 | | Jaimee | 7 |
| Ilka | 6 | | Jami | 6 |
| Ilona | 6 | | Jamie | 2 |
| Imelda | 8 | | Jan | 7 |
| Imogen | 9 | | Jana | 8 |
| Imogene | 5 | | Jane | 3 |
| India | 1 | | Janelle | 5 |
| Indira | 1 | | Janet | 5 |
| Indra | 1 | | Janice | 6 |
| Ingrid | 7 | | Janine | 8 |
| Ines | 2 | | Janis | 8 |
| Inez | 9 | | Jann | 3 |
| Iona | 3 | | Janna | 4 |
| Irena | 11/2 | | Jasmine | 8 |
| Irene | 6 | | Jay | 9 |
| Iris | 1 | | Jean | 3 |
| Irma | 5 | | Jeanette | 8 |
| Isa | 11/2 | | Jeanie | 8 |
| Isabella | 7 | | Jeanine | 4 |
| Isabelle | 11/2 | | Jeanne | 22/4 |
| Isadora | 4 | | Jenelle | 9 |
| Isla | 5 | | Jeni | 2 |

| | | | | |
|---|---|---|---|---|
| Jenna | 8 | Juanita | 22/4 |
| Jenni | 7 | Judith | 9 |
| Jennie | 3 | Judy | 6 |
| Jennifer | 9 | Julia | 8 |
| Jenny | 5 | Julie | 3 |
| Jeri | 6 | Juliet | 5 |
| Jerri | 6 | Juliette | 3 |
| Jess | 8 | June | 5 |
| Jesse | 4 | Juniata | 22/4 |
| Jesseca | 8 | Justina | 22/4 |
| Jessica | 3 | Justine | 8 |
| Jessie | 22/4 | | |
| Jewell | 22/4 | **K** | |
| Jill | 7 | Kacey | 9 |
| Jillian | 4 | Kacie | 2 |
| Jo | 7 | Kaila | 7 |
| Joan | 4 | Kaitlyn | 11/2 |
| Joanna | 1 | Kala | 7 |
| Joanne | 5 | Kali | 6 |
| Jocelyn | 3 | Kalinda | 7 |
| Jodi | 2 | Kallie | 5 |
| Jodie | 7 | Kandice | 11/2 |
| Jody | 9 | Kara | 4 |
| Joelene | 3 | Karen | 22/4 |
| Joelle | 5 | Karin | 8 |
| Johanna | 9 | Karissa | 6 |
| Johannah | 8 | Karla | 7 |
| Joline | 11/2 | Karlee | 7 |
| Joni | 3 | Karlie | 11/2 |
| Jonie | 8 | Karly | 22/4 |
| Josephine | 11/2 | Karmen | 8 |
| Josie | 22/4 | Karoline | 4 |
| Josselyn | 11/2 | Karolyn | 6 |
| Joy | 5 | Kasey | 7 |
| Joyce | 22/4 | Kate | 1 |

| | | | | |
|---|---|---|---|---|
| Katie | 1 | | Kyleigh | 5 |
| Katherine | 1 | | Kylie | 8 |
| Kathie | 9 | | Kym | 4 |
| Kathleen | 4 | | Kymberlee | 6 |
| Kathlene | 4 | | | |
| Kathryn | 7 | | **L** | |
| Kathy | 2 | | Lacey | 1 |
| Katrina | 11/2 | | Laila | 8 |
| Kay | 1 | | Laine | 5 |
| Kaye | 6 | | Lakshmi | 1 |
| Kayla | 5 | | Lana | 1 |
| Kaylee | 5 | | Laney | 3 |
| Keira | 8 | | Lani | 9 |
| Kelley | 7 | | Lanie | 5 |
| Kellie | 9 | | Lara | 5 |
| Kelly | 2 | | Larissa | 7 |
| Kelsey | 5 | | Lark | 6 |
| Kendel | 6 | | Laura | 8 |
| Kendra | 8 | | Laurel | 6 |
| Kerry | 5 | | Lauren | 8 |
| Khloe | 6 | | Laurie | 3 |
| Kim | 6 | | Laverne | 5 |
| Kimberley | 1 | | Lavinia | 5 |
| Kimberly | 5 | | Layla | 6 |
| Kitty | 22/4 | | Lea | 9 |
| Krista | 6 | | Leah | 8 |
| Kristal | 9 | | Lealia | 22/4 |
| Kristen | 6 | | Leanne | 6 |
| Kristi | 5 | | Lee | 4 |
| Kristina | 11/2 | | Leigh | 5 |
| Kristine | 6 | | Leila | 3 |
| Kristy | 3 | | Leilani | 8 |
| Kristyn | 8 | | Leitia | 11/2 |
| Kyla | 4 | | Lena | 5 |
| Kylee | 22/4 | | Lenora | 11/2 |

| | | | |
|---|---|---|---|
| Lenore | 6 | Lorna | 6 |
| Leonore | 3 | Louise | 9 |
| Lesley | 6 | Luanne | 22/4 |
| Leslie | 8 | Lucia | 1 |
| Leticia | 5 | Lucille | 11/2 |
| Letitia | 4 | Lucretia | 8 |
| Lexie | 1 | Lucrezia | 5 |
| Lia | 4 | Lucy | 7 |
| Lianne | 1 | Lydia | 6 |
| Libby | 5 | Lyn | 6 |
| Liesha | 9 | Lynda | 2 |
| Lila | 7 | Lynette | 11/2 |
| Lilian | 3 | Lynn | 2 |
| Lillian | 6 | Lynne | 7 |
| Lilly | 7 | | |
| Lily | 22/4 | **M** | |
| Lina | 9 | Mabel | 6 |
| Linda | 22/4 | Mackenzie | 6 |
| Lindsay | 3 | Maddie | 9 |
| Lindsey | 7 | Maddy | 2 |
| Lisa | 5 | Madelaine | 1 |
| Lisbeth | 3 | Madelene | 5 |
| Lisette | 9 | Madeline | 9 |
| Lissa | 6 | Madelyn | 11/2 |
| Liz | 2 | Madge | 3 |
| Lois | 1 | Madison | 3 |
| Lola | 4 | Mae | 1 |
| Loralie | 9 | Magda | 8 |
| Loren | 1 | Magenta | 7 |
| Lorena | 11/2 | Maggie | 6 |
| Lorene | 6 | Makayla | 1 |
| Loretta | 1 | Malinda | 9 |
| Lori | 9 | Mallory | 6 |
| Lorie | 5 | Mandi | 5 |
| Loris | 1 | Mandie | 1 |

| | | | |
|---|---|---|---|
| Mandy | 3 | Martina | 4 |
| Manuela | 22/4 | Mary | 3 |
| Mara | 6 | Maryann | 5 |
| Marcia | 9 | Maryanne | 1 |
| Marcie | 4 | Marylou | 6 |
| Maree | 6 | Marys | 22/4 |
| Margaret | 11/2 | Masie | 2 |
| Margarite | 11/2 | Matilda | 6 |
| Marge | 8 | Mathilda | 5 |
| Margie | 8 | Maud | 3 |
| Margo | 9 | Maude | 8 |
| Margot | 11/2 | Maura | 9 |
| Marguerite | 9 | Maureen | 5 |
| Maria | 6 | Mavis | 1 |
| Mariah | 5 | Maxie | 7 |
| Marian | 11/2 | Maxine | 3 |
| Mariana | 3 | May | 3 |
| Marianna | 8 | Maya | 4 |
| Marianne | 3 | Meg | 7 |
| Marice | 4 | Megan | 22/4 |
| Marie | 1 | Meggie | 1 |
| Marika | 8 | Meggy | 3 |
| Marilee | 9 | Meghan | 3 |
| Marilyn | 11/2 | Melanie | 5 |
| Marina | 11/2 | Melinda | 4 |
| Marion | 7 | Melissa | 6 |
| Maris | 6 | Melodie | 9 |
| Marisa | 7 | Melody | 11/2 |
| Marissa | 8 | Mercedes | 9 |
| Marjorie | 8 | Meredith | 1 |
| Marjory | 1 | Merissa | 3 |
| Marla | 9 | Merryn | 3 |
| Marlene | 5 | Meryl | 1 |
| Marris | 6 | Mia | 5 |
| Martha | 7 | Michaela | 7 |

| | | | |
|---|---|---|---|
| Michelle | 4 | Nanci | 5 |
| Midge | 11/2 | Nancie | 1 |
| Mildred | 11/2 | Nancy | 3 |
| Millicent | 7 | Nanette | 7 |
| Millie | 6 | Naomi | 7 |
| Mindy | 11/2 | Narissa | 9 |
| Minerva | 1 | Natalia | 22/4 |
| Minnie | 1 | Natalie | 8 |
| Miranda | 6 | Natasha | 1 |
| Missy | 22/4 | Nathalie | 7 |
| Misty | 5 | Nell | 7 |
| Moira | 11/2 | Nellie | 3 |
| Mollie | 3 | Nettie | 1 |
| Molly | 5 | Netty | 3 |
| Mona | 7 | Nevaeh | 1 |
| Monica | 1 | Nia | 6 |
| Monique | 4 | Nikki | 9 |
| Moreen | 7 | Nola | 6 |
| Morgan | 5 | Norah | 11/2 |
| Morgana | 6 | Norma | 7 |
| Morganna | 11/2 | Nova | 7 |
| Murial | 11/2 | Nyssa | 6 |
| Muriel | 6 | | |
| Murielle | 5 | **O** | |
| Myna | 8 | Odessa | 9 |
| Myra | 3 | Odette | 6 |
| Myrna | 8 | Olive | 9 |
| | | Olivia | 5 |
| **N** | | Oona | 9 |
| Nadia | 2 | | |
| Nadine | 11/2 | **P** | |
| Nadiya | 9 | Page | 2 |
| Nadya | 9 | Paige | 11/2 |
| Nan | 11/2 | Paisley | 6 |
| Nance | 1 | Pam | 3 |

| | | | | |
|---|---|---|---|---|
| Pamela | 3 | | Radha | 5 |
| Pammie | 3 | | Rae | 6 |
| Pammy | 5 | | Ramona | 8 |
| Pat | 1 | | Rania | 7 |
| Patrice | 9 | | Raquel | 11/2 |
| Patricia | 5 | | Ray | 8 |
| Patsy | 9 | | Raye | 22/4 |
| Patti | 3 | | Rayna | 5 |
| Patty | 1 | | Rea | 6 |
| Paula | 6 | | Rebecca | 1 |
| Paulina | 11/2 | | Rebekah | 5 |
| Pauline | 6 | | Regan | 9 |
| Payton | 1 | | Regina | 9 |
| Pearl | 7 | | Rene | 6 |
| Peggy | 6 | | Renee | 11/2 |
| Penelope | 7 | | Rhea | 5 |
| Penny | 11/2 | | Rhianon | 7 |
| Peyton | 5 | | Rhoda | 1 |
| Phoebe | 6 | | Rhonda | 6 |
| Phylis | 8 | | Ricki | 5 |
| Pia | 8 | | Riki | 11/2 |
| Polly | 8 | | Rikki | 4 |
| Poppy | 7 | | Rita | 3 |
| Primrose | 5 | | Riva | 5 |
| Priscilla | 9 | | Roberta | 7 |
| Prudence | 5 | | Robin | 4 |
| Prue | 6 | | Robyn | 11/2 |
| | | | Romona | 4 |
| **Q** | | | Romy | 8 |
| Quinn | 3 | | Ronda | 7 |
| | | | Rosalie | 7 |
| **R** | | | Rosalind | 11/2 |
| Rachel | 11/2 | | Rosaline | 3 |
| Rachele | 7 | | Rosalyn | 5 |
| Rachelle | 1 | | Rosalynd | 9 |

| | | | | |
|---|---|---|---|---|
| Rosanna | 1 | | Shanan | 3 |
| Rosanne | 5 | | Shanane | 8 |
| Rose | 3 | | Shannon | 4 |
| Roseann | 5 | | Shari | 1 |
| Roseanne | 1 | | Shauna | 1 |
| Rosemarie | 4 | | Sheila | 9 |
| Rosemary | 6 | | Shelley | 5 |
| Rosetta | 8 | | Shelly | 9 |
| Roslyn | 4 | | Sherry | 3 |
| Rosslyn | 5 | | Sheryl | 6 |
| Roxanne | 1 | | Shiloh | 8 |
| Ruby | 3 | | Shirley | 6 |
| Ruth | 22/4 | | Sibley | 9 |
| Ruthie | 9 | | Sidney | 4 |
| | | | Sienna | 8 |
| **S** | | | Silvia | 9 |
| Sabene | 1 | | Simone | 3 |
| Sabina | 1 | | Siobhan | 5 |
| Sabine | 5 | | Sky | 1 |
| Sabrina | 1 | | Sofia | 5 |
| Sadie | 2 | | Sondra | 8 |
| Sally | 6 | | Sonia | 22/4 |
| Samantha | 5 | | Sonya | 2 |
| Samara | 8 | | Sophia | 5 |
| Sandra | 3 | | Sophie | 9 |
| Sandy | 9 | | Stace | 3 |
| Sara | 3 | | Stacey | 1 |
| Sarah | 2 | | Stacie | 3 |
| Sari | 2 | | Stacy | 5 |
| Sasha | 3 | | Star | 4 |
| Savannah | 8 | | Stefanie | 7 |
| Serena | 8 | | Steffi | 11/2 |
| Serenity | 7 | | Stella | 6 |
| Shana | 7 | | Steph | 5 |

| | | | | |
|---|---|---|---|---|
| Stephani | 11/2 | Teresa | 5 |
| Stephanie | 7 | Terese | 9 |
| Stephie | 1 | Teri | 7 |
| Sue | 9 | Terri | 7 |
| Summer | 8 | Terrie | 3 |
| Suri | 22/4 | Terry | 5 |
| Susan | 11/2 | Tesa | 9 |
| Susana | 3 | Tessa | 1 |
| Susannah | 7 | Thelma | 5 |
| Susanne | 3 | Theresa | 4 |
| Susette | 1 | Tiffany | 9 |
| Susie | 1 | Tina | 8 |
| Susy | 3 | Toni | 22/4 |
| Suzanna | 6 | Tonia | 5 |
| Suzanne | 1 | Tonya | 3 |
| Suzette | 8 | Tracey | 9 |
| Suzie | 8 | Tracie | 11/2 |
| Suzy | 1 | Tracy | 22/4 |
| Sybil | 22/4 | Tricia | 6 |
| Sydney | 11/2 | Trina | 8 |
| Sylvia | 7 | Trinity | 7 |
| | | Trish | 11/2 |
| **T** | | Trisha | 3 |
| Taegan | 3 | Trudi | 9 |
| Tai | 3 | Trudie | 5 |
| Tamara | 9 | Trudy | 7 |
| Tameeka | 2 | Trixie | 4 |
| Tamerra | 4 | Tyra | 1 |
| Tamika | 1 | | |
| Tammi | 2 | **U** | |
| Tammy | 9 | Uma | 8 |
| Tara | 4 | Una | 9 |
| Taryn | 6 | Uria | 22/4 |
| Taylor | 1 | Ursala | 9 |

| | | | | |
|---|---|---|---|---|
| Ursel | 3 | | Wendy | 8 |
| Ursula | 2 | | Whitney | 5 |
| | | | Wilma | 22/4 |
| **V** | | | Winifred | 7 |
| Val | 8 | | Winnie | 11/2 |
| Valencia | 4 | | Winnifred | 3 |
| Valentia | 3 | | Winona | 4 |
| Valentina | 8 | | | |
| Valeria | 5 | | **X** | |
| Valerie | 9 | | Xenia | 8 |
| Vanessa | 9 | | | |
| Vanna | 7 | | **Y** | |
| Vee | 5 | | Yasabelle | 1 |
| Venita | 8 | | Yasmeen | 1 |
| Vera | 1 | | Yasmin | 9 |
| Veronica | 6 | | Yolanda | 9 |
| Veronique | 9 | | Yvette | 7 |
| Vi | 4 | | Yvonne | 5 |
| Vicki | 9 | | | |
| Vicky | 7 | | **Z** | |
| Victoria | 7 | | Zada | 5 |
| Vikki | 8 | | Zahara | 1 |
| Violet | 11/2 | | Zandra | 1 |
| Violetta | 5 | | Zara | 1 |
| Virginia | 8 | | Zelda | 3 |
| Viv | 8 | | Zoe | 1 |
| Vivian | 5 | | Zoey | 8 |
| Vivien | 9 | | Zorah | 5 |
| Vivienne | 1 | | | |

**W**

| | |
|---|---|
| Wanda | 7 |
| Wendi | 1 |
| Wendie | 6 |

# APPENDIX 8

# BOY NAMES WITH
# CORRESPONDING VIBRATIONS

**A**

| Name | Vibration | Name | Vibration |
|------|-----------|------|-----------|
| Aaron | 22/4 | Alastair | 9 |
| Abbner | 7 | Albert | 22/4 |
| Abbot | 4 | Alec | 3 |
| Abbott | 6 | Aleck | 5 |
| Abdul | 4 | Aleksander | 9 |
| Abe | 8 | Alex | 6 |
| Abel | 11/2 | Alexander | 3 |
| Abraham | 8 | Alfie | 6 |
| Adair | 6 | Alfonso | 1 |
| Adam | 1 | Alfred | 1 |
| Adrian | 11/2 | Algernon | 5 |
| Ahmed | 22/4 | Allan | 4 |
| Aidan | 2 | Allen | 8 |
| Aiden | 6 | Alvin | 22/4 |
| Ainsworth | 1 | Ambrose | 1 |
| Al | 4 | Anders | 7 |
| Alain | 1 | Andre | 6 |
| Alair | 5 | Andrew | 11/2 |
| Alan | 1 | Andy | 9 |
|  |  | Angel | 3 |

| | | | | |
|---|---|---|---|---|
| Ansel | 6 | | Ben | 3 |
| Ansell | 9 | | Benedict | 8 |
| Anslem | 1 | | Benjamin | 5 |
| Anson | 9 | | Bernard | 8 |
| Anthony | 7 | | Bernie | 8 |
| Anton | 1 | | Bert | 9 |
| Antonio | 7 | | Bill | 8 |
| Antony | 8 | | Billie | 4 |
| Aram | 6 | | Billy | 6 |
| Archibald | 4 | | Blake | 4 |
| Archie | 8 | | Blaze | 1 |
| Arnie | 11/2 | | Bob | 1 |
| Arnold | 1 | | Bobby | 1 |
| Arthur | 5 | | Boyd | 1 |
| Asher | 6 | | Brad | 3 |
| Ashland | 5 | | Braden | 8 |
| Ashton | 5 | | Bradley | 4 |
| Aston | 6 | | Bram | 7 |
| Austin | 3 | | Brandon | 5 |
| Ayden | 22/4 | | Brandt | 5 |
| Aziel | 8 | | Brayden | 6 |
| | | | Brendan | 4 |
| **B** | | | Brendon | 9 |
| Baird | 7 | | Brent | 5 |
| Barclay | 8 | | Bret | 9 |
| Barlow | 8 | | Brett | 2 |
| Barnett | 8 | | Brian | 8 |
| Barney | 11/2 | | Brock | 22/4 |
| Baron | 5 | | Brad | 3 |
| Barry | 1 | | Broden | 4 |
| Bart | 5 | | Broderick | 4 |
| Bartholomew | 6 | | Brodie | 8 |
| Bastian | 3 | | Brody | 1 |
| Baxter | 7 | | Bronson | 7 |
| Beaumont | 1 | | Bruce | 22/4 |

| | | | |
|---|---|---|---|
| Bryan | 6 | Chadwick | 8 |
| Bryant | 8 | Chandler | 11/2 |
| Bryce | 8 | Charles | 3 |
| Buck | 1 | Charlie | 11/2 |
| Bud | 9 | Chase | 9 |
| Buddy | 2 | Chester | 6 |
| Burgess | 1 | Chris | 3 |
| Burt | 7 | Christian | 11/2 |
| Burton | 9 | Christopher | 4 |
| Butch | 9 | Clarance | 3 |
| Byron | 11/2 | Clarence | 7 |
| | | Clarke | 5 |
| **C** | | Claude | 1 |
| Cable | 5 | Clay | 5 |
| Cal | 7 | Clayton | 9 |
| Caleb | 5 | Cliff | 9 |
| Callum | 8 | Clifford | 1 |
| Calvert | 9 | Clifton | 7 |
| Calvin | 7 | Clinton | 6 |
| Cam | 8 | Clive | 6 |
| Camden | 22/4 | Cody | 2 |
| Cameron | 6 | Colby | 3 |
| Campbell | 1 | Cole | 8 |
| Carey | 7 | Coleman | 9 |
| Carl | 7 | Colin | 8 |
| Carlos | 5 | Collin | 11/2 |
| Carlton | 11/2 | Colton | 7 |
| Carmine | 9 | Conner | 6 |
| Carson | 7 | Connor | 7 |
| Carter | 11/2 | Conrad | 1 |
| Cary | 2 | Conroy | 9 |
| Casey | 8 | Constantine | 8 |
| Cecil | 5 | Conway | 9 |
| Cedric | 6 | Cooper | 9 |
| Chad | 7 | Corbin | 7 |

| | | | |
|---|---|---|---|
| Corey | 3 | Demetrius | 6 |
| Cornelius | 8 | Demitry | 4 |
| Craig | 11/2 | Denis | 6 |
| Crawford | 7 | Denney | 4 |
| Crispin | 7 | Dennis | 11/2 |
| Crosby | 1 | Dennison | 4 |
| Curt | 8 | Denny | 8 |
| Curtis | 9 | Deon | 2 |
| Cyrus | 5 | Derek | 7 |
| | | Derick | 5 |
| **D** | | Dermot | 3 |
| Dai | 5 | Dermott | 5 |
| Dale | 4 | Derrick | 5 |
| Dalton | 3 | Desmond | 11/2 |
| Damian | 6 | Desmund | 8 |
| Damien | 1 | Devin | 9 |
| Damon | 2 | Dex | 6 |
| Dan | 1 | Dexter | 4 |
| Dane | 6 | Dick | 9 |
| Dani | 1 | Diego | 4 |
| Daniel | 9 | Dion | 6 |
| Dannie | 11/2 | Dirk | 6 |
| Danny | 22/4 | Dolph | 1 |
| Daren | 6 | Dom | 5 |
| Darius | 9 | Dominic | 4 |
| Darrel | 4 | Don | 6 |
| Darrell | 7 | Donald | 5 |
| Darren | 6 | Donnie | 7 |
| Daryl | 6 | Donny | 9 |
| Dave | 5 | Dorian | 7 |
| Davey | 3 | Doug | 2 |
| David | 22/4 | Douglas | 7 |
| Davis | 1 | Drake | 3 |
| Dean | 6 | Drew | 5 |
| Demetri | 11/2 | Duane | 9 |

| | | | |
|---|---|---|---|
| Duncan | 3 | Ernest | 9 |
| Dustin | 6 | Ernie | 6 |
| Dwayne | 9 | Erwin | 6 |
| Dwight | 8 | Ethan | 3 |
| Dylan | 2 | Eugene | 3 |
| | | Evan | 6 |
| **E** | | Everett | 5 |
| Earl | 9 | Ewan | 7 |
| Earle | 5 | Ezra | 5 |
| Ed | 9 | | |
| Eddie | 9 | **F** | |
| Eddy | 2 | Faber | 5 |
| Edgar | 8 | Fabian | 6 |
| Edison | 3 | Farley | 4 |
| Edmond | 1 | Faulkner | 7 |
| Edmund | 7 | Felix | 11/2 |
| Edward | 1 | Fenton | 11/2 |
| Edwin | 1 | Ferdinand | 3 |
| Eli | 8 | Ferris | 3 |
| Elias | 1 | Fidel | 9 |
| Elijah | 9 | Finn | 7 |
| Eliott | 9 | Fletcher | 5 |
| Elliott | 3 | Floyd | 8 |
| Ellis | 3 | Francis | 7 |
| Elroy | 3 | Frank | 5 |
| Elton | 3 | Franklin | 4 |
| Elvis | 22/4 | Franklyn | 11/2 |
| Emanuel | 8 | Fraser | 4 |
| Emerson | 8 | Frazer | 11/2 |
| Emmanuel | 3 | Frazier | 11/2 |
| Emmet | 2 | Fred | 6 |
| Emmett | 22/4 | Freddie | 6 |
| Eric | 8 | Freddy | 8 |
| Erich | 7 | Frederic | 5 |
| Erik | 7 | Frederich | 4 |

| | | | | |
|---|---|---|---|---|
| Frederick | 7 | | Graham | 3 |
| Fritz | 7 | | Grant | 6 |
| | | | Grantley | 3 |
| **G** | | | Grayson | 9 |
| Gabriel | 9 | | Greg | 1 |
| Gallagher | 8 | | Gregg | 8 |
| Garcia | 3 | | Gregory | 5 |
| Gareth | 5 | | Greyson | 4 |
| Garner | 9 | | Griffin | 6 |
| Garreth | 5 | | Griffith | 11/2 |
| Garrett | 8 | | Gus | 11/2 |
| Garrik | 1 | | Gustav | 9 |
| Garth | 9 | | Guthrie | 7 |
| Garvey | 6 | | Guy | 8 |
| Garvin | 8 | | | |
| Gavin | 8 | | **H** | |
| Gawain | 1 | | Haden | 5 |
| Geordie | 9 | | Hal | 3 |
| George | 3 | | Hale | 8 |
| Georgie | 3 | | Hamilton | 11/2 |
| Gerald | 11/2 | | Hamlet | 5 |
| Gerard | 8 | | Hammond | 5 |
| Gerrard | 8 | | Hank | 7 |
| Gerry | 1 | | Hans | 6 |
| Gil | 1 | | Hardy | 11/2 |
| Gilbert | 1 | | Harold | 4 |
| Giles | 7 | | Harris | 1 |
| Gill | 22/4 | | Harrison | 3 |
| Gino | 9 | | Harrod | 1 |
| Giovanni | 1 | | Harry | 7 |
| Giuseppe | 8 | | Harvey | 7 |
| Glen | 2 | | Hayden | 3 |
| Glenn | 7 | | Heath | 6 |
| Gordon | 1 | | Hector | 6 |
| Graeme | 4 | | Henri | 9 |

# BOY NAMES WITH CORRESPONDING VIBRATIONS

| | | | | |
|---|---|---|---|---|
| Henry | 7 | Jake | 9 |
| Herb | 6 | James | 3 |
| Herbert | 4 | Jared | 2 |
| Herbie | 11/2 | Jarrod | 3 |
| Herman | 5 | Jason | 5 |
| Holmes | 9 | Jasper | 6 |
| Horace | 5 | Jaxon | 1 |
| Howard | 6 | Jay | 9 |
| Howie | 6 | Jayden | 5 |
| Hugh | 8 | Jed | 1 |
| Humbert | 6 | Jeff | 9 |
| Humphrey | 6 | Jeffrey | 3 |
| Hunter | 5 | Jeremiah | 6 |
| Hurley | 8 | Jeremy | 4 |
| | | Jerome | 3 |
| **I** | | Jerry | 4 |
| Ian | 6 | Jesse | 4 |
| Ibrahim | 6 | Jesus | 11/2 |
| Ignatius | 1 | Jethro | 4 |
| Indiana | 7 | Jim | 5 |
| Irving | 7 | Joaquin | 6 |
| Irwin | 1 | Joe | 3 |
| Isaac | 6 | Joel | 6 |
| Isaak | 5 | Joey | 1 |
| Isaiah | 11/2 | John | 2 |
| Ivan | 1 | Johnnie | 3 |
| Ivers | 1 | Johnny | 5 |
| Ivon | 6 | Jon | 3 |
| Izak | 2 | Jonah | 3 |
| | | Jonas | 5 |
| **J** | | Jonathan | 11/2 |
| Jack | 7 | Jonathon | 7 |
| Jackson | 1 | Jordan | 8 |
| Jacob | 4 | Jose | 4 |
| Jaden | 7 | Josef | 1 |

| | | | |
|---|---|---|---|
| Joseph | 1 | Kirk | 22/4 |
| Josh | 7 | Konrad | 9 |
| Joshua | 2 | Kory | 6 |
| Josiah | 8 | Kris | 3 |
| Juan | 1 | Kristian | 11/2 |
| Judah | 8 | Kumar | 1 |
| Judd | 3 | Kurt | 7 |
| Jude | 4 | Kurtis | 8 |
| Jules | 4 | Ky | 9 |
| Julian | 22/4 | Kyle | 8 |
| Julius | 2 | | |
| Juri | 22/4 | **L** | |
| Justin | 3 | Laine | 5 |
| | | Lance | 8 |
| **K** | | Lancelot | 1 |
| Kade | 3 | Landers | 1 |
| Kale | 11/2 | Landon | 6 |
| Kalleb | 7 | Lane | 5 |
| Kane | 4 | Larry | 11/2 |
| Karl | 6 | Laurence | 7 |
| Karsten | 7 | Lawrence | 9 |
| Keaton | 3 | Lawson | 3 |
| Keith | 8 | Lee | 4 |
| Kelley | 7 | Leif | 5 |
| Kelly | 2 | Leland | 3 |
| Ken | 3 | Lenny | 7 |
| Kendal | 2 | Leo | 5 |
| Kendall | 5 | Leon | 1 |
| Kenneth | 5 | Leonard | 6 |
| Kenny | 6 | Leonardo | 3 |
| Kent | 5 | Leopold | 7 |
| Kevin | 7 | Leroy | 3 |
| Kienan | 9 | Lesley | 6 |
| Kipp | 7 | Leslie | 8 |
| Kirby | 11/2 | Lester | 7 |

| | | | |
|---|---|---|---|
| Levi | 3 | Marty | 5 |
| Lewis | 5 | Marvin | 5 |
| Liam | 8 | Marx | 2 |
| Linton | 3 | Mason | 8 |
| Lionel | 4 | Mathieu | 5 |
| Lloyd | 5 | Matt | 9 |
| Logan | 22/4 | Matthew | 9 |
| Lou | 3 | Maurice | 7 |
| Louie | 8 | Max | 11/2 |
| Louis | 22/4 | Maximillian | 9 |
| Luca | 1 | Maxwell | 9 |
| Lucas | 11/2 | Maynard | 4 |
| Luis | 7 | Mel | 3 |
| Lukas | 1 | Melville | 9 |
| Luke | 4 | Melvin | 3 |
| Lyle | 9 | Melvyn | 1 |
| | | Michael | 6 |
| **M** | | Michel | 5 |
| Mac | 8 | Michelangelo | 5 |
| Mack | 1 | Mick | 9 |
| Mackenzie | 6 | Mickey | 3 |
| Madden | 5 | Mike | 2 |
| Maddox | 7 | Miles | 22/4 |
| Madison | 3 | Milo | 22/4 |
| Mal | 8 | Milton | 11/2 |
| Malcolm | 6 | Mitchell | 1 |
| Manning | 9 | Mohammed | 9 |
| Manuel | 3 | Montgomery | 1 |
| Marc | 8 | Monte | 22/4 |
| Marcus | 3 | Moore | 3 |
| Marion | 7 | Morgan | 5 |
| Mark | 7 | Morris | 2 |
| Marshall | 3 | Morrison | 4 |
| Marten | 8 | Mortimer | 3 |
| Martin | 3 | Morton | 5 |

| | | | | |
|---|---|---|---|---|
| Murray | 6 | Ormond | 7 |
| Myles | 2 | Orson | 9 |
| Myron | 4 | Orville | 3 |
| | | Osborne | 7 |
| **N** | | Osbourn | 5 |
| Nathan | 22/4 | Oscar | 2 |
| Nathanael | 4 | Oswald | 2 |
| Nathaniel | 3 | Owen | 3 |
| Neal | 5 | | |
| Ned | 5 | **P** | |
| Neil | 22/4 | Pablo | 1 |
| Ncill | 7 | Paine | 9 |
| Nelson | 7 | Parker | 6 |
| Neville | 7 | Pascal | 7 |
| Newton | 1 | Pascale | 3 |
| Niall | 3 | Pat | 1 |
| Nicholas | 9 | Patric | 4 |
| Nick | 1 | Patrick | 6 |
| Nigel | 11/2 | Patton | 5 |
| Niles | 5 | Paul | 5 |
| Noah | 2 | Pax | 5 |
| Noel | 1 | Paxon | 7 |
| Nolan | 2 | Paxton | 9 |
| Norm | 6 | Payne | 7 |
| Norman | 3 | Pearce | 3 |
| | | Penley | 5 |
| **O** | | Penn | 22/4 |
| Oakley | 6 | Percy | 4 |
| Oliver | 9 | Perry | 1 |
| Olivier | 9 | Peter | 1 |
| Ollie | 8 | Phil | 9 |
| Olly | 1 | Phillip | 1 |
| Omar | 2 | Pierce | 2 |
| Orion | 8 | Powell | 2 |
| Orlando | 7 | Preston | 8 |

**Q**

| | |
|---|---|
| Quentin | 1 |
| Quinby | 7 |
| Quincy | 8 |
| Quinlan | 7 |
| Quinn | 3 |

**R**

| | |
|---|---|
| Radcliffe | 1 |
| Raja | 3 |
| Raleigh | 6 |
| Ralph | 1 |
| Ralston | 9 |
| Ramon | 7 |
| Ramsey | 9 |
| Randall | 8 |
| Randolph | 7 |
| Ray | 8 |
| Raymond | 9 |
| Rayne | 9 |
| Raynor | 1 |
| Reagan | 1 |
| Redmond | 1 |
| Reece | 9 |
| Reed | 5 |
| Reeve | 1 |
| Reggie | 6 |
| Reginald | 7 |
| Reid | 9 |
| Remington | 7 |
| Renn | 6 |
| Reuben | 11/2 |
| Rex | 2 |
| Rhett | 8 |
| Rhys | 7 |

| | |
|---|---|
| Richard | 7 |
| Richie | 7 |
| Rick | 5 |
| Ridley | 1 |
| Riley | 6 |
| Riordan | 7 |
| Ritchie | 9 |
| River | 9 |
| Rob | 8 |
| Robbie | 6 |
| Robert | 6 |
| Robin | 4 |
| Rodd | 5 |
| Roddy | 3 |
| Roderick | 11/2 |
| Rodney | 9 |
| Rogan | 1 |
| Roger | 9 |
| Roland | 1 |
| Rolf | 6 |
| Rolfe | 11/2 |
| Rollins | 9 |
| Romeo | 3 |
| Ron | 2 |
| Ronald | 1 |
| Ronan | 8 |
| Ronin | 7 |
| Ronny | 5 |
| Rory | 4 |
| Ross | 8 |
| Rowan | 8 |
| Rowland | 6 |
| Roy | 22/4 |
| Royce | 3 |
| Rudolf | 4 |

# APPENDIX 8

| | | | |
|---|---|---|---|
| Rudolph | 4 | Sidney | 4 |
| Rupert | 8 | Simon | 7 |
| Russell | 7 | Sinclair | 4 |
| Ryan | 22/4 | Skip | 1 |
| Ryder | 7 | Solomon | 4 |
| Rylan | 7 | Stan | 9 |
| | | Stanford | 7 |
| **S** | | Stanley | 6 |
| Sam | 6 | Steele | 3 |
| Sammie | 6 | Stephen | 6 |
| Sammy | 8 | Steve | 8 |
| Samuel | 8 | Steven | 4 |
| Sanders | 8 | Stevie | 8 |
| Sandy | 9 | Stewart | 7 |
| Sanford | 5 | Stuart | 9 |
| Saul | 8 | Sullivan | 11/2 |
| Saunders | 11/2 | Sutton | 1 |
| Sawyer | 1 | Syd | 3 |
| Scott | 5 | Sydney | 11/2 |
| Seamus | 6 | Sylvester | 1 |
| Sean | 3 | | |
| Sebastian | 9 | **T** | |
| Selwyn | 8 | Talbot | 7 |
| Seth | 7 | Tate | 1 |
| Shane | 2 | Taylor | 1 |
| Shannon | 4 | Ted | 11/2 |
| Shaun | 9 | Teddie | 11/2 |
| Shawn | 2 | Teddy | 22/4 |
| Shayne | 9 | Terence | 7 |
| Sheehan | 6 | Terrence | 7 |
| Sheffield | 11/2 | Terrill | 4 |
| Shelby | 8 | Terry | 5 |
| Sheldon | 5 | Thaddeus | 1 |
| Shelton | 3 | Theo | 3 |
| Sid | 5 | Theobald | 4 |

| | | | | |
|---|---|---|---|---|
| Theodore | 9 | | Vance | 9 |
| Thomas | 22/4 | | Vane | 6 |
| Thornton | 7 | | Vaughan | 11/2 |
| Tim | 6 | | Vaughn | 1 |
| Timothy | 11/2 | | Vern | 5 |
| Tobias | 3 | | Verne | 1 |
| Todd | 7 | | Vic | 7 |
| Tom | 3 | | Vick | 9 |
| Tony | 2 | | Vince | 8 |
| Torrence | 8 | | Vincent | 6 |
| Trace | 2 | | Vinnie | 1 |
| Travis | 8 | | Vlad | 3 |
| Tremain | 8 | | Vladimir | 7 |
| Trent | 5 | | | |
| Trenton | 7 | | **W** | |
| Trevor | 8 | | Wade | 6 |
| Tristan | 11/2 | | Walden | 5 |
| Troy | 6 | | Waldo | 1 |
| Turner | 6 | | Wallace | 3 |
| Ty | 9 | | Wally | 1 |
| Tyler | 8 | | Walsh | 9 |
| Tyrone | 7 | | Walt | 11/2 |
| Tyson | 3 | | Walter | 7 |
| | | | Walton | 22/4 |
| **U** | | | Ward | 1 |
| Ulric | 9 | | Warner | 7 |
| Ulrick | 11/2 | | Warren | 7 |
| Ulwin | 7 | | Watson | 2 |
| Upton | 5 | | Waylon | 9 |
| Uriah | 3 | | Wayne | 5 |
| Urias | 5 | | Webster | 11/2 |
| Uriel | 11/2 | | Wes | 11/2 |
| | | | Wesley | 8 |
| **V** | | | Whitby | 6 |
| Vail | 8 | | Whitney | 5 |

| | | | | |
|---|---|---|---|---|
| Wilbur | 4 | | **Y** | |
| Wiley | 11/2 | | Yassir | 1 |
| Wilfred | 4 | | | |
| Wilhelm | 1 | | **Z** | |
| Will | 2 | | Zac | 3 |
| William | 7 | | Zachariah | 3 |
| Willie | 7 | | Zacharias | 5 |
| Willis | 3 | | Zachary | 1 |
| Willy | 9 | | Zack | 5 |
| Winston | 6 | | Zak | 11/2 |
| Wren | 6 | | Zane | 1 |
| Wyatt | 8 | | Zeke | 2 |

**X**

| | |
|---|---|
| Xander | 3 |
| Xavier | 7 |